THE IRASCIBLE CHERRY BOMB!
AND OTHER SHORT STORIES

stories by this guy

WAYNE H. BREWSTER

QVI**X**OTE
PRESS

Brewster, Wayne H.
The Irascible Cherry Bomb and Other Short Stories

First edition for Kindle Direct Publishing
Morelia, Michoacán, México. September 2021.

ISBN 979-8-4689-7648-7

© Wayne H. Brewster, 2021
   All rights reserved

Layout design by Qvixote Press
   leo@qvixote.press

Cover design by Óscar Uriel Villalón Jacuinde

The Irascible Cherry Bomb is a work of non-fiction based
on the author's own life experiences. People, places, and events
are generally all real. However, the author embellished
many details to enhance the narrative and do not accurately
represent people's characters, places, businesses,
or real situations. The intent is to entertain rather
than depict reality. All photos included in the book are either
from the author's private collection or from public sources.

For my parents, Harold and Mae Brewster.

Thank you for your role model and life lessons.
I appreciate them every day.

2021

The Irascible Cherry Bomb

No child should ever be allowed to play with explosives! Not ever! However, being a child of the 1950s, that message never occurred to my parents. Firecrackers, and specifically cherry bombs, were a rite of passage during my formative years.

Arizona outlawed all fireworks and firecrackers, so how did I end up with these forbidden incendiary devices? Every summer, my parents and my cousin Truman's parents would travel separately to visit our Kansas relatives. Long before interstates, both families drove US Highway 54 through the Texas and Oklahoma panhandles to and from Kansas. On the trip home, firework stores along this highway became our Mecca. I knew from repeated personal experience that whining and begging were essential to get my father to stop. This activity began as soon as I saw the first billboards advertising these explosive emporiums. Perhaps reluctantly, Dad would stop and allow me a few minutes to shop, supervised by him. We never bought the expensive aerial bombs, but would collect an assortment of Roman candles, sparklers, firecrackers, and a few of the almighty cherry bombs.

My mission accomplished, now I had to get my stockpile home, which involved some subterfuge on my family's part.

In the olden days, Arizona had checkpoints at every highway entering the state to prevent agricultural pests transported into the state. You were to declare any fruit, vegetables, or plants in your possession and hand them over to the agents. *Also forbidden were any fireworks.* My parents were hyper-honest people, so why they allowed those fireworks not to be declared is still a mystery to me. But in our possession and undeclared, they did enter the state.

Safely back home in Glendale, Truman and I would combine our purchases. Then the fun began. We knew the power of those cherry bombs and would devise various tests of their force. The alley, separating my house and my cousin's house, was our testing grounds. It was so cool to blow up potatoes or apples, which became pulverized instantly. Empty cans showed the force exerted on them by bulging in convoluted shapes. Of course, these cherry bombs would make a tremendous racket, and non-enabling neighbors reported us to the police. We only lived a block and a half from the police station, so we had to be agile to escape their investigations. Naturally, we had some close calls, but that never stopped us from continuing our firepower usage.

Once we depleted our stockpile, friends and siblings engaged in other hazardous pastimes. Particularly memorable were the brutal rubber band gunfights, which took place inside my house. Apparently, my mother didn't mind the occasionally broken knickknack or the forts we built with our furniture. Other group activities were the pseudo-sword and dirt-clod fights. I still carry a scar over my left eye where my cousin's wooden sword made contact. My mother almost fainted when Truman rushed me inside, and she saw my blood-covered face. I believe that was the last neighborhood sword fight.

In retrospect, I'm amazed my parents permitted these unsupervised activities. The only warning they ever gave my brothers and me was to stay away from the open, deep, and fast-running irrigation canal that sat across from our house. Shockingly, the other happenings were considered normal kid behavior. I'm happy to report that my brothers, cousin, and I never blew off any fingers due to those irascible cherry bombs. My childhood was long before the United States' 1966 ban on cherry bombs, and life didn't carry omnipresent warning labels. We laughed in the face of danger!

WARNING

EXPLOSIONS IN THE FACE MAY HURT YOU

2010

Books, Food, and Sex: Escapes from Reality!

Author's note: Well, bless my heart! This soap-opera scenario happened while running my retail shop and long before Netflix or owning my Kindle, Firestick, and smartphone. Life was primitive back then! We still had VHS movies, cable TV, and printed books as our only entertainment options. And believe me, that boyfriend didn't last long after this writing! I now refer to this period as Gone With The Wind Down Mexico Way.

Lately, I've been doing a lot of thinking. Surprising, I know!
I process a lot of information daily, but recently, it's been more intense. Life has some grand challenges to deal with, so I've had to re-evaluate the status quo and figure out a new way to proceed. Being a procrastinator, *this is a lot of work and a task I try to avoid.*

During one of those rare thought periods, I realized a startling fact. Three guilty pleasures in my life are directly related. *Books, food, and sex!* I often escape reality by visiting these three related life pleasures. And let's be honest, when each is "executed properly," they can take you to another world. But when they are

The Irascible Cherry Bomb

just ordinary, I tend to think, "I should have had a peanut butter sandwich instead!"

In the interest of decorum, I'll decline to discuss sex other than to quote one of my favorite lines on the subject, "I've substituted food for sex, and now, even I can't get into my pants!"

So really, what I want to discuss with you are books and food. When the two blend together under the same cover, it's a marriage made in heaven.

English language books are hard to come by here in the heart of provincial Mexico. You obtain them via friends' gracious gifting and re-gifting practices or by ordering them directly from the US, which is very expensive. So during the recent visit of my former wife, Peggy, and her friend, Pam, they gifted me several books.

Pam was so kind as to give me *Mexico*, by James A. Michener. My goodness, this man knew how to construct stories spanning centuries and generations of characters. And if you've read his epic novels, you know that he was extremely detailed in reconstructing history to fit his storyline. I highly recommend this fictional account of Mexico's passage from a violent indigenous culture to a violent European/indigenous culture. And along the way, you will learn all about the art of bullfighting, not that I attend many bullfights, but if I did, I would know the difference between a *muleta* and a *capote*.

Then my current (and to remain nameless) paramour loaned me one of his books, Eckhart Tolle's *A New Earth: Awakening to Your Life's Purpose*. Well, reading this self-help book every night out loud to my paramour gives me a headache. I must be clueless, but I can't quite get how I'm supposed to enter a new consciousness level by reading this book. I understand the author's premise that "things" tie us to the shallow ego. Releasing our attachment to "things" will allow us to progress to a newfound spirituality and a higher consciousness level. But my goodness, I make a living by selling things to people that makes them feel good. What would happen if the entire world gave up this 'shallow" form of consumerism? How would we all survive? Don't we need the income that this consumerism provides billions of people worldwide? We can't go back to the jungle or live off the land to find personal happiness in a new awareness. I mean, isn't Eckhart Tolle making money off selling a book that is a "thing" based on consumerism? What a bunch of crap! And the entire time, my paramour is saying, "See, I told you!" Well, maybe he won't be so arrogant if I took away those 350 TC sheets he is sleeping on or the comfortable couch he is sitting on while watching the History Channel on my new high-definition television. Now *there* is a new reality!

Peggy gave me the perfect combination of literature and food. *Insatiable,* by Gael Greene, former food critic for *New York Magazine,* and it's a sheer delight to read. It's naughty, brilliant, funny, and *"an aphrodisiac for the soul."* I can't put the book down. It incorporates her sexual adventures with her culinary experiences. In her own words, *"for me, the two greatest discoveries of the twentieth century were the Cuisinart and the clitoris."* Gosh, I wish I'd been wise enough to pen that. And all through the book are fun, exciting recipes that she collected and used during her life.

I want to share one of Gael's recipes as a tribute to my former wife. Growing up in Phoenix during the mid-20th century, blueberries and I never met. I don't remember eating blueberries until I started dating Peggy. One of her fondest childhood mem-

The Irascible Cherry Bomb

ories was visiting Massachusetts every summer with her mother and going out to collect wild blueberries. And through Peggy's love of this berry, our kids and I developed a passion for everything blueberry.

Gosh, that's a long way to go to share a recipe with you all. I hope you enjoyed the journey.

Blueberry Pie with Orange-Nut Crust

- Crust:
    2 cups flour
    ¼ tsp. salt
    2 tsp. sugar
    8 oz. unsalted butter
    2 tsp. grated orange rind
    1/3 cup finely chopped almonds or pecans
    5 tbsp. ice water
- Filling:
    4 cups blueberries
    ½ cup sugar
    2 tbsp. cornstarch

Preheat oven to 375 degrees. If you have a pizza stone, place it on the bottom rack.

Mix flour, salt, and sugar in the bowl of an electric mixer. Cut butter into eight pieces. Using the paddle attachment, add one piece at a time. Continue processing until pieces of butter are no larger than a pea. Add orange rind and nuts and process briefly. Remove bowl from the mixer.

Sprinkle three tablespoons of the water over the mixture and mix all with a fork. Pinch the dough together. If it holds and doesn't feel dry, you don't need to add the remaining water. If it's dry and does not hold together, add remaining water, one tablespoon at a time, as necessary to make the dough come together. Roll into two balls, flatten, and wrap separately in plastic. Refrigerate for approximately one hour.

Remove one pastry disk from the refrigerator 20 minutes before rolling. Roll the pastry and line a nine-inch pie plate with it. Refrigerate the pastry-lined dish and remove the remaining pastry disk from the fridge while preparing the berries.

Pick over the berries, then gently toss with granulated sugar and cornstarch. Pour into pastry-lined pie plate.

Roll out remaining pastry. If you have a lattice-top form to punch out a checkerboard top, use it. Otherwise, cut 3 to 4 slits in the top layer of pastry once you have laid it over the blueberries. Moisten the edges and crimp to seal.

Place on the bottom rack of the oven, ideally on the pizza stone. Bake for 20 minutes. Reduce temperature to 350 degrees and move the pie to the middle rack and bake for another 20 minutes. The pie is done when the juices start to bubble, and the crust is nicely browned on the edges. Serves 8.

2020

Car Issues

My good friend Sid and I have very little in common. We met almost thirty years ago in Phoenix, Arizona, and since I've moved to Michoacán, Mexico, he's been my most frequent visitor. Our friendship resembles *The Odd Couple* movie, as we've very few similar interests. I love to cook, and he only has a kitchen because it came with the house. I love watching televised singing competitions, and he loathes them. I call a plumber, and he repairs the issues himself. He enjoys camping, while I love glamping. I, at best, take cars for granted, and he loves to collect them. It's my car issues with Sid that I wish to discuss.

From the moment that I pick Sid up at the Morelia airport, I have car trouble. It happens all the time! It's a recurring joke to everyone who knows us. They ask me, "What happened to your car this time?" Usually, it's mundane things like a tire goes flat, the car overheats, or an automatic window stops working. My car can be functional and problem-free until Sid gets in, and then all hell breaks loose. I call it our 'carma.' Some of the more harrowing experiences are local legends, which my friends retell every time Sid visits.

Let's be fair. There were four years that I drove a junker. It was a 1993 Toyota Camry. Driving this car was humbling. I felt like Goofy in one of those cartoon jalopies bouncing down the road with the doors banging open and closed. The suspension was non-existent, and it was notorious for scraping every speed bump it met. However, it did manage to get me safely from point A to point B—that is, at least until Sid would arrive.

One day, we drove an hour to Santa Clara del Cobre (center of Mexico's handcrafted copper arts) so that Sid could buy a copper tabletop. As we arrived back in Morelia and stopped at the first stoplight, fumes started spewing from under the hood. Sid pointed out the obvious to me, and not wanting to panic, I said calmly, "Not to worry. There's an AutoZone just around the corner, and we can get help there." I drove the one block with plumes of steam streaming through the open car windows while Sid grabbed the passenger door in anticipation of having to execute a tuck and roll. Sid assumed a mechanic's role in the parking lot and opened the hood to see the issue. A busted radiator hose.

Well, that would be easy peasy to fix. We entered the store to explain our dilemma and to buy a replacement hose. (I'm not

The Irascible Cherry Bomb

sure why Sid went into the store with me since he only knows one Spanish word, *entonces,* which means so or therefore. Maybe it was for moral support or to show me his superior auto mechanic knowledge.) As luck would have it, they did have the correct replacement hose. When we got back to the car, the part wouldn't fit since it had an extra bend. I went back inside and got one of the employees to come out and see the problem. She assessed the situation, pulled out a knife the size of a Ginsu cleaver, and cut off the contested part. Issue solved. Sid's mouth flew open, and his eyes bugged out, not believing what just happened.

I laughed and said, "Hey, get a grip! You're in Mexico, and we know how to work around problems. It's called *Mexicanada,* doing crazy things that somehow work."

I casually added. "I've done my part, and I'll leave you to install the hose. While you're doing that, I'm going to the grocery store to do a little shopping." For some reason, Sid found fault with my thinking. It made perfect sense to me. We both were doing tasks within our wheelhouse.

One day, we decided to drive to Patzcuaro, a magical town, less than an hour from my home. Sid inspected the tires and the thin tread on them because I had asked him naively, "Do you think these tires will make it to Patzcuaro and back?" He rolled his eyes and replied, "You may make it to the tire shop before we have a blow-out!" Sarcasm is one of his most charming characteristics. I huffily said, "You do realize that it would cost me $15 to $20 to buy a slightly used tire. Let's stop and make sure the air pressure is correct, and we should be fine!" And they were fine—that is, until they weren't.

Wayne H. Brewster

One day, Sid noticed that my muffler was dangling below the bumper like some pinata at a kid's birthday party. Being rather mechanical, he rummaged through my "Barbie" toolbox, moving out of the way my glue gun collection, three dozen glue sticks, and assorted-color florist wire reels, and he spied three wire-plate hangers. He asked me, "Can I use one of these plate hangers to reattach the muffler to the car's frame?" Panic-stricken, I replied, "No. I might need it, and I could never find a replacement here in Mexico." Sid prevailed, and that muffler stayed in place thanks to a 99 cent plate hanger—that is, until it didn't.

On another occasion, Sid and I joined some friends attending the annual Geranium Festival in Tingambato, a beautiful historical village an hour away from Morelia. Our first stop was for lunch at La Mesa de Blanca, a destination restaurant located in another country town near Tingambato. To access their parking lot, you must drive up a short but steep cobblestone ramp to park under the shade of some fruit trees. After lunch, two ladies joined Sid and me in my car, and I took the lead in going down the slope to the road. Horrible scraping sounds and vibrations were originating from the bottom of my car. I stopped and got out of the car to see what had happened. There lying exposed, like a giant dead anaconda, was my entire exhaust system. It had been ripped off my car by the stone ramp, due to my faulty suspension and the extra two-person weight. My friends expressed their shock and disbelief but began laughing to relieve the tension. I, too, started laughing. There was no way to save the exhaust system, so I dragged it out of the way and left it for someone to collect and make a few pesos from recycling. And I never did find the plate hanger. We proceeded to the Geranium Festival

The Irascible Cherry Bomb

with exhaust fumes flooding the interior and a deafening sound that threatened to cause permanent hearing loss. Driving back to Morelia that evening was challenging due to the loud noise, toxic fumes, and cold air whipping us through the open windows. One of my passengers was a Canadian who was visiting Mexico for the first time. I think this experience frightened her so much that she has never returned for another visit. Her reaction still mystifies me.

I can hardly wait for Sid to visit again. My mechanic looks forward to his visit as well. He wants to add a new room to his house!

2021

Cartalk

To say I find no exhilaration in car ownership is a gross understatement. I'm one who believes a vehicle is a money-sucking and exhaust-belching necessity in need of constant repair. Undeniably, there are demented car people that *LOVE* their cars. Ho-hum. It's beyond me why some people happily collect cars. I know some therapists that can cure you of that addiction.

The only time I genuinely got a woodie over a car was when my father purchased a 1959 Oldsmobile Super 88. Look at those hot rocket fins! It was so other-worldly compared to the tacky, faded-green, post-war, 1950 Dodge we owned. This new car magically transformed us from poor white-trash to the modern middle-class gentry. I felt like a youthful prince riding in that Oldsmobile, and I would yell and wave at friends on the street to let them know how cool I was. This car was sleek, modern, air-conditioned, plush, and fast as any car on the highway. You might label it a tank, but it had mid-century panache!

The Irascible Cherry Bomb

I've personally owned many cars in my lifetime. Some were luxurious, some were utilitarian, and some were horrible! My first car was a 1963 Valiant, and I would categorize it as utilitarian. My father purchased it for me when I graduated from high school in 1965 to have transportation to college. It had an old-church-lady white exterior, faded-lipstick-red interior, on-the-column manual transmission, and cost my father a whopping $700. It was bare-bones practical and provided me with dependable yet classless transportation for six years. I should mention that it didn't have air-conditioning, and the Phoenix summers brought home that fact. It was a sweat-mobile rather than a cool Batmobile. Oh, the stories I can and will tell about this Valiant.

Shortly after our June 1969 wedding, Peg and I moved to San Francisco, where I secured a job with a local department store in their executive training program. Of course, that Valiant went with us. It was a blistering hot, two-day journey from Phoenix to San Francisco, and adding insult to injury, the car broke down on the highway as we entered Livermore, California. With my minuscule knowledge and disdain for auto mechanics, I was clueless. What to do? I thumbed a ride to a repair shop while leaving Peg to sweat in the car in 100-degree heat. We learned the U-joint boot cover needed replacing after towing the Valiant to a garage and reviving my heat-stroked bride. I didn't know that a universal joint existed or even wore boots.

After an hour or so delay, we arrived in the cool city by the bay. We were so happy and excited about our new life adventure. Our destination—a pseudo-Chinese-style, furnished Russian Hill apartment—sat at Union Street's crest. Our little Valiant tried vainly to make it up Union Street. We quickly realized that it hated hills and refused to climb them, stalling midway up the steep incline. Now I was sweating bullets as I blocked horn-honking, finger-thrusting traffic to turn around and find a new route to our home. We learned to circumvent the steep streets for another year or so by snaking our way up those storied hills.

One year later, I received a promotion to manage the men's casual wear department in the Emporium's Terra Linda, Marin County store. Peg was working in the city, and we chose not to move to the suburbs. This decision meant I had to commute over the Golden Gate Bridge to and from work. The commute was easy, as I was going against traffic. My only complication was concerning the Valiant's trunk and not carting store merchandise in the said trunk. You ask why? Sometime before, the trunk's lock had fallen out, and I replaced it with a wire hanger. Lordy, I was clever! This arrangement worked fine except when I was crossing the Golden Gate Bridge. The crosswinds created a sort of mini-tornado in my trunk, causing the parcel shelf in the back seat to flap up and down, along with the trunk's cover banging open and closed. All that was missing was a banjo-playing soundtrack. Adding salt to my wounds, my then boss, Dan Long, would tell everyone at the store about my hillbilly Arizona car and then laugh hysterically. That same year Peg and I bought a new Audi SL100, which ended the rude and humiliating comments.

The Irascible Cherry Bomb

The saddest and yet funniest story concerning the Valiant was after we had purchased the Audi. By this time, we had moved from the semi-classy highrise apartment to a funky flat with a garden and single-car garage located on Russian Hill's charming Russell Street. Of course, the Audi got parked in the garage while the Valiant sat on the street in front of our building. Shortly after that, a neighbor stopped me and told me the police had hauled away our Valiant for violating the 72-hour street parking limit. What? Sure enough, the Valiant was gone, and we never missed it! So the next day, I went to the closest police station and told them my situation. The policeman presented me with a massive bill of $300 for towing, storage, and a fine. Damn that Valiant! It was causing me to sweat bullets again as I didn't have the funds to pay that bill. My brilliant mind quickly formed the question, "What if I just leave the car and don't pay the charges?" The policeman smiled and said, "I think we can work something out." He explained that if I signed the title over to him, he would take care of the charges. Done deal! What a sad ending for my first car. Oh, well, moving on.

In 1972, we decided to move back to Phoenix to start our family. The Audi came with us, but it lacked air-conditioning, so I traded it for an Audi Fox. It was air-conditioned but hardly cooled the interior during the intense Phoenix summers. In 1976, we bought a Buick Century. It was a great car that served our young family for years, and the air-conditioning worked. God bless American-made cars! We drove the wheels off that car since we lived across town from my job. Peg needed the car many days, we'd load the kids in the back seat and drive to Scottsdale, and then she would return to Glendale. Repeat the trip at night. Our small children, Lauren and John, ate so many meals in the back seat that the fabric was permanently stained and gave off a lingering peanut butter aroma.

The cars we drive say a lot about us—Alexandra Paul. If that's true, then I need a life redo!

2011

Weather or Not

Today is a blustery day in central Mexico, with the sun and passing clouds playing a game of peek-a-boo. This dramatic scene of light and shadow conjures up memories of similar days in Phoenix, my previous home.

Pacific winter storms would sweep through from the west, dumping snow and rain throughout Arizona. But it was always the day after these storms when the winds would come and give our desert paradise a taste of bone-chilling cold weather. So we desert dwellers would bundle up in our most bulky sweaters and jackets like we were living in Buffalo, New York.

This week, the U.S. news has been full of reports concerning the winter storm of the decade. I read and watched this news in both amazement and wonder while I smugly basked in sunny day after sunny day. I've always been a weather freak, and the perfect days in Morelia create a longing for a taste of winter weather. I remember past years when Phoenix weather brought me new experiences and excitement.

I must have been about eight years old or so when I saw snow for the first time. Snow in Phoenix is almost as rare as the proverbial hen's teeth. It was a Saturday morning, and I had awakened earlier than my parents. Looking out my bedroom window, it was a gray, still morning. I got out of bed, put on my old wool robe and fuzzy slippers, and slipped quietly out into the backyard. It felt warmer than it should have. I sat on the edge of our picnic table and turned my head skyward. All of a sudden large white flakes began falling from the sky. I jumped up in disbelief and ran to tell my parents the news, "Mom! Dad! It's snowing!" They, of course, weren't as excited as I was since they had experienced snow and blizzards of their Kansas youth. But, to me, it was a revelation. And as quickly as the flakes appeared, they disappeared. But for a few precious moments, I experienced the joy of snowfall.

Later, Mom related a day during the late 1930s or early 40s when there was accumulation, and my eldest brothers got to have snowball fights in our front yard. If only I had been alive to see that! Snow continued to make rare appearances during my adulthood. It snowed on Christmas Day in 1974 and then again just before Christmas Eve day in 1990. My family and I have since had the joy of White Christmases in Germany and northern Arizona, but those rare Christmas days in Phoenix still hold a special place in my heart.

In December 1967, Arizona must have experienced an *El Niño* effect, long before this terminology existed. For eight days, it rained in the desert and snowed non-stop in higher elevations. Five to eight feet of snow buried Arizona's high country. After Christmas, my father gave me the task of going to Prescott to check on our cabin. My parents were very concerned to know if it was still standing under the weight of all the snow. I asked a group of friends to accompany me and help clear off the roof (if there was a roof). When we arrived in Prescott, there was so much snow that the streets were small tunnels. There was no way to clear the roads entirely, which left snow walls towering over each lane eight to ten feet high.

The county had plowed the forest roads to a few permanently occupied houses, but we had to walk a short distance to our cabin. The snow was so deep that the landscape lay blanketed in a soft downy mantel. It was slow and arduous going as you would continuously break through the surface and plunge downward several feet. We finally made it to the cabin, and it was still standing! I remember making a fire in the fireplace, but it was so cold inside the fire provided little warmth. We were able to get on the roof effortlessly due to the high drifts packed against the house. It didn't take us long to clear the roof. As we were leaving to return to Phoenix, I remember trying to forge a little creek in my car. The frozen surface gave way, and my right rear wheel became stuck. Regardless of how much I tried, it would not come loose. I had to walk to a house a short distance away and beg the owner to use his truck to get us free. My lack of experience in hazardous, winter-weather driving was clearly to blame for our predicament. The joy of being liberated to continue our journey back to Phoenix helped overcome my embarrassment.

One winter day, when I was in fourth grade, I awoke to an incredibly foggy morning. I hadn't seen fog of this intensity or density previously. Walking to school was otherworldly. All of the usual and familiar sights were shrouded in dull, fuzzy light. Visibility continued to disappear as the morning progressed. I remember distinctly being on the playground and not being able to see more than a few feet. It wasn't frightening, as once again, it was a new experience and provided my childhood life with excitement. Naturally, as the sun increased its climb into the midday sky, the fog burned off. I have since experienced fog in many exotic places—San Francisco, Italy, London, and mountain passes—but none of them compare with that foggy morning when I was ten.

Then there were the Salt River hundred-year floods in back-to-back years from 1978 to 1980. The normally dry river bed that runs diagonally through metropolitan Phoenix became a raging torrent, which divided our city into two isolated zones. Unfortunately, I lived in Mesa's Dobson Ranch (southern zone), and my office sat in Scottsdale Fashion Square's Goldwaters (northern zone). Typically, this was a thirty-minute drive back and forth, but this journey took anywhere from an hour and a half to three hours each way during the floods. In 1978, only three bridges spanned the Salt River—the old Tempe Mill Ave. Bridge, Central Ave. Bridge, and the Maricopa Freeway bridge. Well, the floods took out the freeway bridge, so that left just two bridges available for traffic to pass back and forth between north and south zones. It was a nightmare that lasted for six weeks. Emergency construction of new bridges allowed the following two year's floods not to paralyze the city. Today, newcomers to Phoenix wonder why there are so many bridges crossing a dry river bed. I lived through the reason.

As I look out the window of my new Mexican existence, the clouds have increased, and the shadows have lengthened. But the nostalgia I feel transports me back to winter days in Arizona. It's a journey that warms my soul.

June 6, 2021

A Meaningful Historical Date

Today, June 6—a historic day for me and the world. Most people associate it with the anniversary of D-Day in World War II. And every year, I, too, remember the brave Allied forces who invaded Europe fighting for freedom over Fascism. So let's explore the personal reasons I celebrate this day.

Most importantly, it is my wedding anniversary. On June 6, 1969, I married Peggy Curran in Mount Carmel Catholic Church, Tempe, Arizona. It was a stiflingly hot June evening ceremony with me sweating profusely either from nerves or the weather. At least I didn't faint or mess up the vows. A reception followed, catered, and hosted by Peg's mother. Marge, Peg's mother, had worked endless hours making the bridesmaid's dresses, a three-tier beautiful wedding cake, and all the food and beverages served. Whew, I'm exhausted just writing about it. She was a force of nature, my mother-in-law. Peg and I had a lovely honeymoon in San Francisco. You know the type of thing: cable cars, Chinatown, Fisherman's Wharf, and all the other tourist attractions we could fit in a week's stay. We also had to look for an apartment as I had accepted a position with The Emporium

Department Stores beginning in August. These events started a twenty-two-year marriage, which produced two beautiful children and some incredible memories. The marriage ended, but the friendship and bond still tie us.

Two life-long friends celebrate their birthdays on June 6. June Masters and I were in side-by-side cribs every Sunday while our mothers took active roles in Glendale, Arizona's First Methodist Church. So we genuinely are life-long friends. Likewise, Ed Berberian and I became best friends through the same church attendance, high school, university, and our mutual years living in San Francisco. Both of these friends remain close in my heart and thoughts. I wish they would come to visit me for a long-overdue reunion.

Then twelve years ago today, I left Phoenix for a new life adventure in Morelia, Michoacán, Mexico. It was a big move, but one I have never regretted. The night before, my friend Donna Everett Valdez hosted a going away party that saw so many friends and family attend to bid farewell. It was a cherished memory and an emotional moment in my life. Kerry Bedwell and I hopped into my overloaded Jeep Grand Cherokee the following day and headed south towards the final Mexican destination, not knowing what the trip would bring. It was a three-day trip that Kerry continues to complain about as butt-numbing. The only highlight of the tedious drive was having a wonderful seafood lunch in Mazatlán.

Kerry was the obvious choice to accompany me on this trip. We had become best friends through meeting thirty years ago in Phoenix's gay men's chorus. Sharing similar approaches to life, we set a course of friendship that survives to this day. But, oh,

The Irascible Cherry Bomb

lordy, we have had our share of adventures and disagreements. Kerry and I, mostly Kerry, produced three weddings together that were spectacular. In addition, he helped stage two milestone birthdays for me and many celebratory dinners. The list of mutual accomplishments and collaborations is too long to detail. The only time he wanted to kill me and end our friendship was working on a critical feature of my business' trade show booth. I had the brilliant idea to turn my trade show booth into an Italian market. It had market umbrellas, green market aprons for all the workers, logoed Kraft-paper shopping bags, and a stuccoed wall running through the center of the two-sided booth. It was truly spectacular, and we did win several best of show awards with this design. However, the key feature was a tiled roof that capped the stuccoed wall. We couldn't use actual roof tiles as they would be too heavy for the Styrofoam faux stucco walls. So Kerry came up with the fantastic idea to take Styrofoam cups, cut them in half, and glue them to foam sheets to create the look. Well, we built this booth and roof in the blazing hot Phoenix summertime. My obsession with getting the tiles looking perfectly aged pushed Kerry's volcano to erupt. I've never heard such language before in my life. He let me know that my opinion and direction were not needed or appreciated. However, once we cooled down, all was forgiven, and a funny memory exists today, like our friendship.

What a special day this is to look back and celebrate!

Wayne H. Brewster

June 6, 1969—left to right: Marge Curran, Peggy Curran Brewster, Wayne Brewster, Mae and Harold Brewster

Kerry Bedwell in Mazatlán, June 7, 2009.

The Irascible Cherry Bomb

The infamous Styrofoam cup roof—team members: Ky Milliron, Sid Foutz, and Jeff Connit.

The finished trade show booth.

2020

Watch out for falling cows!

You don't hear that every day!

On a recent trip driving along the California coast, my former wife Peg asked me, "Did I dream it, or did a cow fall off a hill and almost hit our car years ago?" I thought to myself, "Perhaps it's time to look for some permanent care for this woman." Keeping my voice restrained, I answered, "Gee, I don't recall that happening during our time together. I think it was someone else in your life." Then our son John and I broke out in uncontrollable laughter. After all, what are the chances of a cow falling on your car? So, Peg whipped out her phone to Google "falling cows" and to save a bit of face in the process. Apparently, this phenomenon of falling cows is a real issue in California and has happened multiple times. CalTrans has posted highway warning signs on SR-178 & Old Kern Canyon Road, where there have been numerous instances of cows falling off hills, hitting cars, or being hit by motorists. It is a free-range area for cattle, and when it rains, the grass on the steep hills gets slick, and the cows tend to slide down the incline and tumble onto the roadway.

The Irascible Cherry Bomb

So, the moral of the story is that pigs don't fly, but cows do fall! "Watch out for falling cows?" Only in California!

Photo courtesy of roadtripamerica.com.

2019

Christmas Musings

This past weekend, Peg, my former wife, and I reminisced about Christmases past and our favorite ones. We laughed over Christmases when our children, Lauren and John, were youngsters, and the gifts that made a hit or didn't. The disappointing Barbie townhouse we gifted versus the dream house our daughter wanted. Star Wars action figures that started a lifetime collection for our son. The Cabbage Patch doll year when there were none available, and then a neighbor found us one. The dreaded hamsters both kids wanted and received.

Then each of us related childhood Christmases that remain vividly engrained in our memories. She recounted fondly one Christmas morning while living in South Dakota when she received a special doll and many other gifts that she had wanted. I remember the year Santa brought me a cage of parakeets and a game where you shot corks at metal ducks as they were twirling on a tripod, two very creative gifts from my practical parents. *My standard Christmas gifts were sox and underwear! Ugh!*

We both agreed that the best Christmases were when our little family traveled to Germany, a white Christmas in Greer, Arizona, and a Prescott, Arizona cabin nestled in the pines. Those times seemed less stressful, more relaxing, and ultimately more fun. Sure the snow and cold weather helped, but it was the quality time with our family that made it special.

As I age, Christmas brings out conflict in me. I've always said that I enjoy the preamble to Christmas more than the actual day. You're probably wondering, "How can that be?" It's simple. I much prefer the preparations over the big event. What that says about me is open to debate. But decorating the house, putting up the Christmas trees, and shopping gets my endorphins going more than any exercise ever could! Christmas Day seems somehow anti-climatic to me.

Growing up, my family celebrated the holiday on Christmas Eve with the extended family. The emphasis tended to be more on the family gathering and a special dinner. Gifts were secondary. Then Christmas Day was a downer as there was nothing but another family gathering and dinner. Once I met Peg and was involved in celebrating the holiday with her family, it was Christmas overload. Tons of gifts on Christmas morning. Peg holds on to that tradition as she buys twenty gifts for each family member, and you can barely walk into the room because gifts clog the way. It is a bit overwhelming. Perhaps, those combined experiences explain my enjoyment of pre-Christmas to the day's reality.

You see, I have a personality that tends to overdo everything, and when it comes to preparing for Christmas, it ain't pretty. For many years I was determined to write and send hundreds of Christmas cards to everyone I knew. This task had to be completed by December first to be first out of the pack. I got tired of that game somewhere around the turn of this century. Then I started writing Christmas letters as a creative exercise that mocked the more traditional ones. In one of them, I mentioned that I was a spy in Mexico and went to prison for smuggling in sea salt to the US. Well, that ended when some gullible people on my mailing list took me seriously—imprisoned for sea salt? Really?

Because of my professional background in buying, selling, and merchandising Christmas decorations for retail and wholesale, I love to decorate for the season. Or should I say overdecorate for the season? It borders on obsessive-compulsive behavior. I have a storage room filled to the brim with three large trees and dozens of tubs holding all the ornaments, lights, garlands, and accessories. I brought many of these items with me when I moved from Arizona to Mexico, which nobody in their right mind would do. The term downsizing isn't part of my vocabulary. *(I've known people who told me to rid myself of this clutter, so I defriend them on social media. Problem solved!)*

The entire process takes a week to install all the décor. I used to do it myself, but I've hired exceedingly patient young Mexican men for the last few years to assist me. Unfortunately for them and me, they've never decorated a tree in their lives. This fact causes me to lose my temper and voice while making the festive installation less than joyful for those involved. Oh, please don't shame me. They're paid generously for this abuse. Merry friggin' Christmas!

I always start with the living room tree. This tree is almost twenty-years-old and has seen better days. Initially, it was pre-lit, but several years ago, one of my elves had to cut off all the no longer functioning lights. Now we have to restring the lights. This past year, I had to break in a new sprite. It took this young man

The Irascible Cherry Bomb

half a day and three attempts to figure out how to get the lights on the tree and to my perfectionist satisfaction. Then the rest of the day to decorate the tree in its frosted white and silver theme. It was a work of art, and you can't tell the actual tree is held together with wire and hot glue.

The recently purchased seven and a half foot upstairs tree is a breeze. You insert the three sections, and *voilà*, the lights come on with sixteen different, remote-controlled color combinations. Additionally, I string three or four strands of bubble lights that create movement and a festive mood. I use this tree to hold my Mexican theme of red, green, and white ornamentation and with Mexican flags fluttering here and there. I have to admit it is festive, and my guests tend to love it, which makes me happy. I work in old family ornaments into the trees as these mementos bring me intense joy in remembering special people and their association with the holidays.

For example, two unique Christmas cards that my Grandma Brewster gave me over sixty years ago have places of honor on my tree. I have two tin cones that graced my childhood tree, which are getting a little battered, like me. I have a blue and silver bell-shaped ornament that existed on my Uncle Loren's tree from the same era. Some of the more unusual items on the tree are a Stars and Stripes-design Mickey Mouse head purchased at Disneyland, a red and black plastic cowboy boot bank given to me when I was six by my Aunt Hazel, and a brightly painted glass bust of Frida Kahlo.

Once we've completed both main trees, we move on to other interior decorations and the outside. Everywhere you look, something is sparkling or blinking at you. It is a lot of work, but I enjoy that special feeling of the season for a month. All the glitter and tinsel brings me joy and comfort since I'm not usually with family on this holiday. So the simple moral of the story is, enjoy this time of year doing something that makes you happy. But along the way, remember special people and special times because that's what adds value. Merry Christmas from my house to yours!

The Irascible Cherry Bomb

Wayne H. Brewster

2019

Want List

You people north of the border (NOBs) haven't a clue! You all live in the Almighty Land of Commercialism and have *everything* you could want or need within a small circumference of your home. However, for us living in Tortillalandia, hunting and gathering is a serious, time-consuming business. We may visit a dozen stores looking for a critical ingredient and come up empty-handed. Heartbreaking!

Laugh all you want. I don't give a flying squirrel what you think! The other day, I was walking my local Walmart's aisles when I spied Hormel Chili! I stopped dead in my tracks. To you, it may seem ordinary, but for me, it was almost like discovering the Holy Grail. I scooped up four or five cans, as you never know if they will appear again on the shelves. Once in 2017, I found a giant-sized can of Bush's Baked Beans. I'm hoarding it until there is a special occasion to merit its usage. Heck, a few months ago, I found mint jelly in a store. I bought it, and I don't even like or use mint jelly. Then recently, I found Pillsbury Crescent Rolls. So, of course, I bought them - as the last time I saw them locally was ten years ago. I served them to my local friend, Arnold Garcia, and explained why this was a special occasion. He appeared blasé after my gushing explanation. Somehow I remember them tasting better, which means the excitement of discovery is more satisfying than the result.

Living in Mexico, we ex-pats spend a lot of time searching for products originating from back home. It's comforting to feel that connection. For example, I subscribe to Sunset Magazine and love their recipes. Again, it's for comfort and connection. However, when I read the list of ingredients, half of them I've never heard of and the other half I'll never find locally. I made one recipe that called for fennel pollen, dandelion greens, lovage, and Piave cheese. What? So I substituted bee pollen, arugula, cilantro, and queso fresco. Yuck! Those creative substitutions became instant garbage.

Each time I visit the US, I return home to Mexico with bulging suitcases filled with ingredients impossible to find here. Horseradish, chili powder, dry mustard, brown sugar, butterscotch chips, smoked paprika, and the list goes on. There is a glimmer of hope that this laborious process will eventually stop. Little by little, imported products appeared on local store shelves. I remember when I first arrived in Morelia, I couldn't find real lemons. Lots of limes but no lemons. Now you can find them everywhere. Recently, half-and-half appeared in the dairy aisle. Can buttermilk be far behind?

Times are changing! This October, a new super gourmet store opened in our beautiful city. It borrowed the Whole Foods store concept and offered us a delightful, upscale shopping experience. My first visit was a blurred outing for all the tears in my eyes.

2013

Clueless!

After years of therapy, I've learned not to point out my friends' foibles, but this story is just too good to pass up. So, forgive my backsliding!

I've had repeat visitors to my Morelia, Mexico home over the years. Since I live in the state of Michoacán, "The Soul of Mexico," there is an overabundance of culture, history, and beautiful scenery, and I try to expose my visitors to this bounty. Several years ago, I took a friend on an outing to Quiroga and Tzintzuntzan, two fascinating towns near Morelia. We had a lovely day visiting many of the tourist shops that comprise Quiroga. We dined on carnitas at El Rey de Carnitas in Quiroga's central plaza. Afterward, we visited Tzintzuntzan's Straw Market and the historical church grounds. While we were in Tzintzuntzan, I decided to show my friend the Tarascan archeological ruins that overlook the town. After driving up the hill, we pulled off the road to the ruins' entrance, and I took photos for several minutes, leaving my friend on his own. I then asked, "Would you like to go inside the park?" He answered, "No, I've seen enough. Is that all there is to it?" I acknowledged that the view included mostly everything there was to see. I was surprised but didn't think much about it at the time.

Fast forward to a week later. Two local friends accompanied my friend and me on another outing to visiting near-by artisan towns. We stopped by a Capula ceramic factory, which I had previously investigated as a potential source for my export consulting business. I decided the factory was not a suitable candidate. Then onward to lunch at an El Tigre restaurant. During lunch, I asked the group what we should do for the rest of the day. The conversation ensued that perhaps we should revisit Tzintzuntzan since my friend didn't see the whole town. My friend brought up the fact that he had a postcard of some Tarascan ruins, and they were much larger than the one I had shown him earlier. All of us jumped in, saying that there is only one group of ruins in Tzintzuntzan, and if he saw them the first time, he had pretty much seen all of it. He replied, "Well, I want to see them again because they are much larger than what you showed me the first time! I won't say any more until we are there!" Okay, so off we went.

Again, we visited the Straw Market, the churches with their extensive grounds, and then off to the ruins. I stopped my car in the same place we had the previous week and pointed to the ruins. "See my friend. There are the ruins!" He said, "NO! You told me that this was the ruins on the other side of the road!" We all turned to see what he was looking at, and it was a house under construction! He thought the house was the ruins! We were all dumbfounded and speechless! I said undiplomatically, "How could you possibly believe that a house with bricks and concrete were Pre-Columbian ruins?" Clueless!

The Irascible Cherry Bomb

Can you tell the difference?

2020

Dining Out - Deprivation and Recovery

I suffered a sad, deprived childhood because my father adamantly disliked dining out. His gastronomic apathy caused me profound emotional issues, which stunted my gourmet pubescence. Therefore, as a precocious child, I rarely experienced those mystical places called restaurants, cafes, diners, and coffee shops. Oh, there were the rare exceptions when my family traveled across the country, and Dad acquiesced to eating out. I remember once me begging him to stop at a Howard Johnson's on the Blue Ridge Parkway, He reluctantly did, and I felt thoroughly vested in American consumerism.

On another occasion, Dad and our family had to dine in a New York City restaurant. It was a hot and humid, late-August 1953 evening, and we were visiting the Big Apple for the first and only time. We stayed at the iconic Art Deco-style Empire Hotel on West 63rd Street. I'm foggy on the details if we dined at the hotel's restaurant or another nearby. However, I do remember very well the altercation with the restaurant's maître d'.

My father was not suitably dressed, since he wore what you would call Arizona dressy casual: dress slacks and a short-sleeved

The Irascible Cherry Bomb

shirt. The maître d' forbid him to enter the restaurant without wearing a sportcoat. Never mind that the weather was stifling and the restaurant was on the balmy side—he had to wear a jacket. Standards had to be maintained! Dad had some harsh words for this New York City-arrogant-unbudging-dandy. The negotiated cease-fire allowed Dad to wear one of the restaurant's on-hand jackets. He reluctantly agreed so as not to disappoint his mother and aunt accompanying us. Dad looked like a cooked turnip in a heavy tweed sport coat, but the dinner proceeded with only an argument between Dad and my Aunt Rena over bill-paying rights. I have no recollection of what I ate but remember feeling somehow very sophisticated. Imagine, I was just a few days from entering first grade, and I was dining in a fancy NYC restaurant. Unfortunately, this pretentious twit had to sleep on three side chairs pushed together to create my bed. A humbling experience that no way dampened my memory of my first taste of the Big Apple.

The New York Incident happened because every summer during the 1950s, Dad would pack the family into our old, humpbacked, green, 1950 Dodge, affectionately called The Turtle, and we would head east from our Glendale, Arizona home. Most of the time, my Grandmother Brewster would join our family of six. You might wonder how seven people could fit in that car. It wasn't easy. My seat assignment was upfront sitting on Mom's hard-as-a-rock cosmetic case. My brother Ron also sat upfront between Mom and Dad while my other two brothers and Grandma rode in the back seat. Ron's feet had no place to go except my youthful backside. To avoid the bruises and to see anything of the countryside, I had to stand up. Therefore, you could say I stood up for America.

Of course, the car had no airconditioning, so we would head out very early morning to miss the heat driving through the shimmering Arizona desert. These trips were long before interstates existed, and we would take U.S. Highway 60 through Mesa, Superior, Globe, and the dreaded Salt River Canyon to reach cooler climes.

Show Low, Arizona, a rough-and-tumble lumber town in eastern Arizona's White Mountains, was our habitual first stop. Breakfast was the main priority at a rustic café that is long gone, and its name not remembered. I always ordered the short stack of buttermilk pancakes, which, to this day, are my standard. They were delicious! Another recollection was my mother's coffee cream delivered in those sealed, adorable porcelain miniature creamers. Porcelain creamers make more sense today versus the ugly plastic pods. Why can't we return to this chic container instead of the trashy substitute?

These annual trips across the U.S. broadened my palate preferences. They allowed me to experience delicious regional foods. I tried hush puppies in Florida, red beans and rice in Louisiana, fried catfish in Mississippi, fried okra in Kansas, real maple syrup in Vermont, and muskmelons in Ohio. These revelations converted me from a limited kid-diet of tomato soup, peanut butter and jelly sandwiches, or grilled cheese sandwiches. A foodie was being born.

Meanwhile, in Glendale, we had limited dining options. The best choices were two Mexican cafes—La Perla and La Cocina—both now closed and only exist in my memory. La Perla Cafe,

The Irascible Cherry Bomb

family-owned, survived 70-years and was a legendary Glendale café. My first visit was on Mother's Day 1956, when mom refused to cook, and the extended Brewster family gathered there. The beautiful smells emanating from the kitchen linger with me to this day. However, as my tastebuds matured, I preferred the littler and quainter La Cocina, as the food seemed fresher and more authentic. My dear lifelong friend, June Masters, and I would go there quite often for lunch during our teenage years. The standard fare included my favorite safe combination of hard shell beef taco, bean tostada, and cheese enchilada served with rice and refried beans. During one visit, I do believe it was the first time I ever ate a cheese crisp. It's an Arizonan invention of a sizeable open-faced flour tortilla (the size of a large pizza) that has been brushed with butter and covered with shredded cheese, then broiled to its crispy perfection. If you haven't tried one, it could be life-changing.

During high school, my friends and I would cruise Phoenix's Central Avenue on Saturday nights. The place to go and be seen was Bob's Big Boy on Thomas Road and Central. It was *Grease* and *American Graffiti* in real life. Despite all the social interaction activities, they had the best food: Big Boy hamburgers, French fries, onion rings, cherry and vanilla-flavored Cokes, and "super thick" milkshakes. It was American diner food, but it had *je ne sais quoi*. I always felt sorry for the waitresses who worked there since they had to take abuse from hormonal teenage customers dished out in abundance. To compensate, I tipped generously, probably 25 cents. Hey, don't laugh; that's when a quarter would buy you a gallon of gasoline.

As my parents aged, even they began to broaden their dining-out horizons, and being the last child at home, I too benefited from this cultural shift. Due to Glendale's restaurant void, they naturally turned to Phoenix, where there were countless great places to eat. When the out-of-town company arrived, they preferred to give them some local color. Pinnacle Peak and Reata Pass Steakhouses offered mesquite-grilled steaks along with some contrived cowboy charm. It was a long trek to get there, thirty-five miles northeast from downtown, but they were fun places to visit. The huge cowboy steaks were delicious and worth the long drive.

My initial fine-dining education falls securely at the feet of two relatives. For a month each spring, my older second cousins, Zell and Jo Smith, would visit from Bakersfield, California. They belonged to the country club set and loved frequenting Phoenix's swanky restaurants. Being an adorable, overindulged, red-headed lad, I was naturally their favorite, so I got to visit many places far off my parent's radar. They introduced me to some then glamorous venues that added a level of experience. For example, they often stayed at downtown Phoenix's Sahara Motor Inn, where I, a good Methodist,

The Irascible Cherry Bomb

met George Gobel in the bar where he was smoking and drinking. I got his autograph despite his sinful behavior. We dined at the Flame Restaurant and Rooster Bar in downtown Phoenix with its dark and smokey ambiance, along with their jungle bar décor. It was a perfect Rat Pack setting, and I'm sure we were rubbing elbows with Mafia members. Several times we had lunch at the Venetian Terrace, an elegant, white-linen, chichi restaurant perched on the eighth floor of midtown's Mayer Central Building, across from Park Central. It was there that I drank a Shirley Temple cocktail for the first time, or maybe it was a Roy Rogers. Thankfully, it didn't turn me into an alcoholic! Open for several years; the location morphed into Phoenix's Playboy Club. Other places crowd my memory, but I'm always grateful to Jo and Zell for taking me under their wing and educating me on a different life than I was leading.

I must mention an iconic Arizona café, which captured my heart all those many years ago. Before it became I-17, the smaller Black Canyon Highway opened in the 1950s, which allowed us to discover an old stagecoach stop café and bar. It oozed pure history and western charm. Driving north, we would always stop at Rock Springs Café for breakfast or on the way home for pie or sometimes both. Their breakfasts were delicious, and their pies legendary. Plus, it was a historical building that, until recently, had not been overly gentrified. Of course, like everything in our world, it has changed under new ownership, but I still stop there in homage to its former status.

I feel blessed that my professional and personal life allowed me to travel extensively throughout Europe, the South Pacific, Mexico, and the United States. These trips presented unlimited opportunities for fine dining and new culinary experiences. I've grown from the tomato soup kid to a lover of many cuisines, but I still have my limits. Just don't try to make me eat liver and onions. Yuck!

La Perla Café, Glendale, Arizona.

Hotel Empire, New York City.

Sahara Motor Inn, Phoenix, Arizona.

The Irascible Cherry Bomb

The Flame and Rooster Bar, Phoenix, Arizona.

Wayne H. Brewster

Sahara Motor Inn, Phoenix, Arizona.

The Irascible Cherry Bomb

Reata Pass Steakhouse, Scottsdale, Arizona.

Bob's Big Boy, Phoenix, Arizona.

WAYNE H. BREWSTER

Rock Springs Café before gentrification.

2020

Tik Tok or Not

Friggin' Millennials and technology! They think they're so bright because they were born with a cellphone in their hand. Humph! I can butt dial with the best of them.

Contrary to our stereotypical misconception, my age group didn't arrive in this world in a covered wagon or a Model-T Ford. Let's get real! In my case, it was a faded, navy-blue 1936 Chrysler sedan that brought me home from the hospital. I was born in 1947, which makes me a proud Baby Boomer. In my early life, standard communication methods consisted of letter writing and one old-fashioned telephone, which sat on a small hallway table in my childhood home.

Oh, dear, I do sound pathetically pioneer. Never mind! My age isn't the issue! What's warranted is an affirmation of my lifetime technology usage.

Let's start by commenting on our family's only telephone. That big, black Bakelite phone connected my family to the outside world. My father ran his successful painting and decorating business using that phone. Unfortunately, he had a bad habit of scribbling significant telephone numbers on the wall surrounding it, which he justified by saying, "I know where to find the number when I need it." You can see by that personal detail we weren't upper-class.

Customers could only solicit Dad's professional services by phone, so I had to be careful about how I answered the phone. Since being a child prodigy of politeness and manners, I used this greeting, "Hello, Brewster residence." Yes, I know. Precocious and just a wee bit pretentious.

Of course, we had a party line. (I should explain this concept to the younger folk reading this esposé. A party line existed when two or three families shared the same telephone line. Shocking, right?) And if you wanted to make a call, you had to wait until the other parties hung up. God forbid if you wanted a private conversation with a friend or girlfriend as everyone on the line or in the house was privy to what you were saying. So I learned to speak in code during my teen years.

I've failed to mention that there existed only one phone company for the entire United States. AT&T provided this service until Congress broke their monopoly, and our local system became U.S. West. In those days, you didn't own your physical phone but rented it. I imagine this trivial tidbit shocks the younger crowd.

My mother purchased a more modern touch-tone phone with an unusually long cord after my father passed away. God forbid she would install extension phones. The long cord allowed her to move the phone to her desk or family room and not have to run to answer it. I remember our first home telephone number was only three digits, 651, later it became YEllowstone7-7836, and finally 602-937-7836.

The Irascible Cherry Bomb

Oh, and by the way, our first phones were rotary dial. You had to literally stick your index finger in the numbered holes and force it clockwise till it stopped. Then, select the first number and dial, then the following number, and dial. Repeat eight more times. It was exhausting, but it's how we kept our fingers limber back then. Push-button phones came much later, as did cordless ones. Once again, I'm a technological pioneer.

Even with a phone, people took the time to write letters in cursive. My Aunt Margie, my third-grade teacher, played a pivotal role in this regard; she made our class practice the Palmer Method of cursive writing every day. Today, I'm thankful for those lessons and maintain beautiful penmanship. (Haha! I've got one up on those Millennials because I can read and write cursive, and they can't. Sorry, I couldn't resist throwing shade on those young 'uns!)

Back to writing letters, you didn't call a loved one or friend in another state or town unless it became an absolute emergency. You sent them a note because a stamp cost three cents, and the United States Postal Service delivered mail every day except Sundays! And you knew your postman by name and gave him a Christmas present every year.

I still have a collection of these epistles sent to me by family and friends. Today, reading them brings back a simpler life when you discussed all your activities, but never anything too personal. I loved my mom's letters. She'd write about the meals she prepared, her garden, her church involvement, and what each of her sons was doing. For example, she'd tell me, "I did two full clotheslines of wash today." Or, "I fried a mess of fish yesterday for supper. Had Grandma and Aunt Margie in for dinner, and they said it sure was good." Even if those details seem mundane by today's standards, you won't believe the joy of receiving mail. Today, I'd panic if I received a mail-delivered card or letter. "Oh, no! Who died?"

During high school, I took typing lessons in Mr. Morgan's class. Not being particularly coordinated, I never mastered this skill set. Probably in my senior year, my parents gave me a portable manual typewriter. Since I was a terrible typist, I made a lot of errors. Time and time again, I would stop and have to correct my mistakes. Luckily, I discovered onionskin paper, which allowed you to erase your mistypes easily. The only other alternative was to use a quick-drying white coverup fluid and then, once it dried, retype over the problem. Of course, your finished product was bumpy and spotted. Neatness did matter, but what could I do? I should have bought stock in Liquid Paper. During my junior and senior college years, I was editor-in-chief of Arizona State University's yearbook. By that time, I had graduated to an electronic typewriter. Did my skill set improve? Marginally, at best.

The electronic revolution entered during the 1960s. Around 1968 while attending ASU's College of Business, I had to do a class assignment using a mainframe computer. Lord have mercy, I had to type a sequence of punch cards and then feed them into the machine to produce a report. You guessed it; my typing errors screwed up the final paper. But the point is older people, like me, have been adapting to new technology their whole lives and still are.

The Irascible Cherry Bomb

Laugh, if you want. As a department store buyer, I remember when I procured my first hand-held calculator—what a gift from the gods that was. It cost a lot, but it made my life so much easier. Before then, we had to extend our purchase orders by hand. In the 1980s, I bought my first computer to help run my sales business. We had one of those noisy dot matrix printers with the carton of folded paper fed into the machine. It performed the task efficiently, cheaply, but slowly compared to today's laser or inkjet printers. I did master that computer and then, later on, the wonderful world of Microsoft programs and the World Wide Web.

Who can remember when I got my first cell phone? Probably in 1999 or 2000. Up until that time, we used landlines and payphones. I remember having my business phones billed through a new start-up company offering cheaper tolls for long-distance than our local provider. They also provided me with my own 800 number that customers could call. When on the road selling or attending national shows, I could dial into one of their 800-numbers and enter a code and then dial anywhere in the U.S. without having to use a credit card or coins to make calls. I thought I was so cutting edge.

Fast forward to today. Technology rules our lives. If you don't believe me, then ask Alexa. That know-it-all bitch controls everything and eavesdrops on all our conversations. "Alexa, turn on downstairs lights. Good morning, Alexa, and good morning to you too, National Security Agency." I do like Alexa's playlists, so I'll keep her around for a while. She can also answer all my questions and tell me jokes. Now I can permanently put my brain in neutral. Thanks, Alexa.

WAYNE H. BREWSTER

Next issue! Is it just me, or are you also bothered by the over-abundance of communication tools we have? It's all justified by making our lives more comfortable and more productive, but I find it's damn annoying! I have a local landline phone, a separate phone for my MagicJack (VoIP) Arizona number, computer, tablet, and a multinational cellphone with various apps—Messenger, WhatsApp, Facebook, Gmail, and Instagram. I've even dabbled in Skype, Zoom, and other video calling programs for business, family, and friends. Then I have countless options for my evening viewing pleasure: cable (yes, I still have it); a U.S. television viewing app; a loaded Firestick with Netflix, Acorn, YouTube, and the Prime Video app. And some friends have firmly suggested that I watch TEDtalks and podcasts. I would rather slash my wrists than watch those laborious programs. It's to the point of over-kill. Chirps, rings, dings, pings, and buzzes constantly interrupt my life until I want to cover my head with a pillow and scream. This digital revolution is turning me into that cranky old man who those Millennials ridicule. Hell. Let them have Tik Tok, Twitter, Tumblr, WeChat, Snapchat, Reddit, and Viber. Who needs them?

Here's the deal. Technology is great and wonderful and provides instant gratification. However, the downside is impaired interpersonal skills. Have you ever tried to have a face-to-face conversation with a Millennial? It's impossible. They can't look you in the eye for more than a few seconds because they're focused on their hand-held device pinging out messages to them. On the other hand, I love meeting people and having lengthy conversations over coffee, wine, or meals. It's more human than texting a person at the same table and having them reply in return. Hello, that's what we call polite conversation. It's more fulfilling and nurturing than any GIFs or emojis. Will future generations go mute because they've lost the ability to communicate verbally? Paraphrasing a Mr. T quote, "I pity the fools!"

Studies show that Millennials read more books than their parents. Now that surprises me. Therefore, the chances are good that a Millennial will stumble upon this book and read this essay. So first of all, thank you! But understand this point, one day, you will be my age, and there will be new technology that you'll struggle to learn or disdain. You're walking the same path as us Baby Boomers have. We're all pioneers in our times, and we have to adapt to survive and thrive.

See. It was an old faded Chrysler sedan. I'm the little guy standing in front of my family, circa 1949.

2018

Rethorical Questions

Aging is one of life's cruel hoaxes. One's mind and spirit don't mature at the same rate as one's body. Metaphorically speaking, a person in their golden years often looks like a cantaloupe left too long to ripen, but once cut open, their interior still is firm, sweet, and succulent. As I've advanced through the years, my body has morphed into some frightening act of nature while my brain tries to convince me I'm thirty-something. Have you had a similar experience?

Here's another bitch slap in the face. Once you hit that senior-citizen point-in-life, you realize you don't have all the answers anymore. When I was younger, it seemed like I had answers for everything. This senior phase is starting to piss me off!

I want to air my dirty laundry list of questions that I can't seem to answer. Any input would be appreciated.

1. Why is it that when I do laundry, one sock out of a pair goes missing? What happened to the missing sock? In false hope, I have a drawer full of single socks waiting for its mate to reappear. They never do.

2. Why have they made electronic devices smarter than their senior owners? Most of the seniors I know have our local and saintly tech guy on speed dial. He's such an essential factor in my life that he's on retainer. His first kind question is always, "Have you thought to shut down and restart your device?" Uh, no. He is so patient with me!

3. Why is it that I can sit all day with no visitors and no phone calls when my cell and landline ring at the same time while someone is knocking at the door? Does the universe tell everyone to drive Wayne crazy at that precise moment?

4. Why is it when you want to introduce one of your best friends to someone, you can't remember their name? I can remember my second-grade teacher's name and her street address, but I can't remember my best friend's name. What the heck?

5. Why do I take the time to prepare a shopping list and realize that I've left it on the refrigerator upon reaching the grocery store? Then, when I return home and check, I find that I haven't bought a single item that I needed.

6. Why am I always attracted to someone who has absolutely no interest in me? Pathetic.

7. Why didn't I listen to my parents more? Finally, I realized their advice was right on too far into my adulthood.

8. Why didn't I prepare for retirement better? See question number seven.

9. Why do I go to find something, and when I get to where I'm going, I can't remember why I'm there? Dementia, short-term memory loss, or just old age?

10. Why is it that I can't remember where I parked the car when I go to a mall or big box store? Thank god for car key fobs and their ability to signal the car alarm.
11. Why is my bed more welcoming than going out with younger friends to a bar? The dread of the following day and the two days of recovery?
12. Why have I've recently developed ADHD? For example, I'm cooking dinner, then go to check out my Facebook account. Then stop and start folding the laundry I left several hours ago. Oh, the garden needs watering. Finally, the screaming smoke alarm brings me back to the original task. Oh, damn it! Blackened tilapia is not a new recipe I wanted to try.
13. Why have Netflix and Prime become my only passionate nighttime visitors? See the over-ripe cantaloupe reference above!

2010

Day of the Dead

Autumn has finally arrived in central Mexico, a subtle seasonal shift different from North America's northern climates. The days are shorter, and at our high altitude (6,300'), the weather has turned more refreshing, with the nights almost chilly and requiring a light sweater. The daily rains have departed, and the impotent clouds dotting the evening sky are a brilliant sunset display of fiery oranges, reds, and pinks set against a royal purple background. The countryside has turned from the emerald green of summer to subtle gold and orange, with grasses and cornfields maturing after their season of bounty. Everywhere new flowers have started blooming, signaling a new phase of nature's annual calendar. Vast banks of lemon-yellow and gold sunflowers reach for the sun. Wild tiny marigolds inflict their spicy scents upon the breezes and compete for space in the fields of magenta cosmos, yellow asters, and goldenrod. Brilliant white displays of daisies and Texas olive trees in full bloom now dominate the hillsides. The native ash trees have started showing yellow tinges in their lush crowns. But the most apparent sign that fall has arrived is the celebration of the *most Mexican* holiday, Day of the Dead.

Morelia and towns surrounding Lake Patzcuaro are the epicenters of this annual ritual. I feel blessed to live here, but especially during this time of year.

A floral parade of pickup trucks has rushed down our streets full of orange marigolds, delicate baby's breath, and dark purple cockscomb. Their fragrant loads destined to be sold by street vendors. Every business has constructed elaborate displays of prayer candles, sugar skulls, and the intricately crafted *banderas picadas* or paper fiestas flags. Catrinas, in fanciful dress, appear everywhere as the iconic symbol of Day of the Dead. This preparation is for the oldest holiday on this continent, celebrated continuously for over 3,000 years. The Aztecs began this special day in remembering their dead every August. When the Spanish conquered the New World, the Catholic Church tried to end this pagan ceremony but instead decided to incorporate it into the celebration of All Saints Day (Nov. 1) and All Souls Day (Nov. 2). Thus, this ancient festival took place in the first two days of November for almost five hundred years. And as a direct link to its indigenous heritage, the decorated sugar skulls of the current celebrations represent actual human skulls' usage in their ritual.

Throughout Mexico and parts of the U.S, people prepare elaborate altars within their homes, businesses, or at the actual grave sites to welcome the spirits of departed loved ones to return for one night. Whether it is an altar within the home or the cemetery, much time and care make the display unique and personal. First, tombs are painted or scrubbed clean. If there is no tomb, then the earth is turned and mounded to replace what the summer rains have washed away. Then personal keepsakes, photographs, favorite beverages, and food are added to the deceased's tribute. The final and most elaborate touch is the floral display. Many are intricate and take hours of collective work: crosses with loved one's names, shapes of churches, angels, and humorous ones of cars or bicycles. The usage of orange marigolds is dominant in almost all displays. The belief is that this traditional flower's scent reaches the departed in the spirit world and draws them to the grave or altar. The petals of the flowers are stripped and scattered over the surfaces, somewhat like confetti. The vital use of favorite beverages and food is so that the spirits can eat and drink after such a long journey. The entire family spends the day preparing the gravesite and then spends the rest of the night watching and waiting for the loved ones to appear. Candles are integral to the displays, and their smoke spirals upward towards heaven like arms trying to bring the spirits to earth. This intimate night-long vigil is more upbeat than a sad event with laughing and reminiscing, all fueled by food and *cerveza, tequila, pulque,* and other regional beverages. It's a true celebration of life, while acknowledging death is part of it. It's magical to behold and, once viewed, impossible to forget.

The Irascible Cherry Bomb

Wayne H. Brewster

The Irascible Cherry Bomb

Time of publishing update: Unfortunately, a negative aspect occurred after the 2017 release of the Disney movie *Coco*: visitors by the tens of thousands descended upon our environs. Tour buses now clog the country roads to the point of night-long traffic jams. It's changed the locals' desire to visit the villages during this rite.

Household Tips and Other Tips

Taken verbatim from the First Methodist Church's 1948 W.S.C.S Cookbook, Glendale, Arizona

No embellishment is necessary as they are priceless!

- You can give extra gloss to linoleum by adding a little clothes starch to the mop water.
- To keep lard from splattering while frying, sprinkle a little salt.
- When driving a nail into plaster, first rub it on a cake of soap.
- Spots may be cleaned from hats by rubbing corn starch into them and then brushing gently.
- Hat veils may be ironed by placing between sheets of waxed paper.
- An apple cut in half and placed in the cake box will keep the cake fresh several days longer.
- Ice trays will not stick in the refrigerator if, first, you set it on a piece of waxed paper in the freezing compartment.
- To keep small rugs from slipping on polished floors, sew old fruit jar rings to each corner underneath.
- Protect your curtains in the washing machine by first placing them in a pillow slip.

- String beans will be easier to string if crisped in the refrigerator a few hours before stringing.

Tips for the Stout Woman

- Avoid dainty and spindly chairs and furniture, which serve to accentuate your bigness.
- Hats with wide and slanting brims are usually best.
- Use a medium-size handbag, preferably square or rectangular. Too small a bag emphasizes your stoutness, and too large a bag may look too bulky.

Tips for the Tall Woman

- Always wear your hair as flat as it can be made on top.
- Long-haired furs are very suitable.
- Never make the mistake of trying to walk or stand in a slouched or bent over position in an effort to minimize your height.

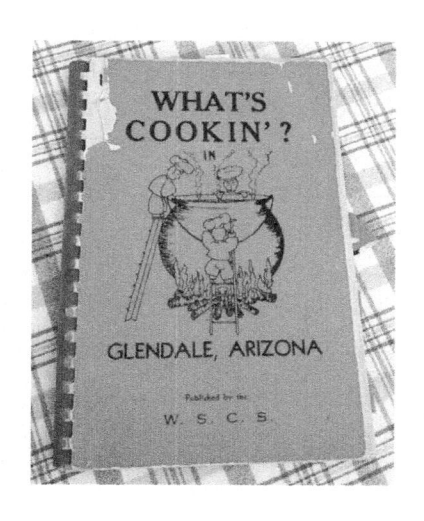

2011

Dreaming of Paradise

Helen Keller said, *"The most beautiful things in the world cannot be seen or even touched; they must be felt with the heart."* Her quotation expresses my feelings for one of the most beautiful and cherished places of my youth. It was our family's rustic cabin near Prescott, Arizona.

Our cabin sat within the Prescott National Forest, off Iron Springs Road, and a mere six miles west of the town center. It lay tucked in an isolated dell, with lush ponderosa pines, gamble oaks, and scrub chaparral blanketing the surrounding small hills. Perennial Spence Creek ran through our property's center, flanked by verdant cottonwood trees that would quake and whisper in the gentle daily breezes. Huge granite boulders were scattered across this land, adding character to the idyllic scene with the challenge to climb and conquer. The dwelling provided our family shelter but was virtually derelict and lacked any modern conveniences, yet it was our family's private paradise!

Almost every summer weekend, we would make the two-hour journey northward from Glendale to Prescott via the historic US

The Irascible Cherry Bomb

89 that snakes its way up the side of Yarnell Hill. In those early, pre-airconditioned Arizona days of my youth, we would anxiously count the miles as we left our scorched desert valley and spotted the first ponderosa pine that signaled cooler mountain air. The trip was always an endurance adventure in our old '50 Dodge, which the family affectionately nicknamed *The Turtle* for its sun-faded, dull green paint, and domed-shaped body. Each Friday morning, Mom would pack *The Turtle* too full of people, pets, and provisions and then leave late morning before the hottest part of the day. Generally, our father would drive up in his truck on Friday night after work, so the packing and hauling fell to Mom by default. It is a family miracle—or maybe due to our mother's iron-maiden personality—that we managed to survive those sweltering trips without a meltdown.

To break the monotony of these weekly journeys, we would recite the same historical facts concerning the sights along the way. In Wickenburg, we would encounter our first trivia site, the Hassayampa River. We always pointed out its ironic sign stating that it was illegal to fish from the bridge. You might ask, "Why is that an ironic sign?" Because the desert river is dry most of the year, and there are no fish to catch! Obviously, Wickenburg's city fathers had a sense of humor. Then there was the famous fable that if you drank the water from the Hassayampa River, you would never tell the truth again. I'll let you determine if I did or didn't drink that water!

Our last famous Wickenburg landmark of note was the Jail Tree in the center of town. As the story goes, Wickenburg didn't have a proper jail, so that the local sheriff would chain up the criminals to a big old mesquite tree. That 200-year-old mesquite is still alive and serves as a visual warning to those modern-day cowboys intent on tearing up the town to mind their P's and Q's.

Leaving Wickenburg and heading up the White Spar highway to Prescott, you would drive past the old gold mining town of Congress, which consisted of a few wooden shacks, a saloon, and numerous rusted, abandoned cars. We smugly labeled any fool who chose to live in those God-forsaken places Desert Rats, not acknowledging that we were of a similar demographic. But one of our favorite landmarks was the brightly painted Green Toad, balanced precariously on the side of Yarnell Hill. It was an enormous granite boulder that did indeed resemble our amphibian friends. Some of Congress's good citizens decided to paint it, so there was no mistaking the resemblance. My teetotaler mother would often whisper to other adult travel companions that some saloon patrons initiated the idea to paint the rock. I had little understanding of alcohol's potent effects at my tender age, but it seemed like an excellent idea to me!

Once you arrived in the small town of Yarnell, you knew that the worst of the heat was over. And if you felt like praising God for this deliverance, you could always stop off at the serene Shrine of St. Joseph, a religious park, to say your prayer of thanksgiving. One of the most scenic areas on this highway is the bucolic Peeples Valley, just a few miles north of Yarnell. This area exemplifies our image of an Old Western landscape. Ranches sporting white wooden fences circling their acreage fill the valley. The lush green pastures support grazing herds of cattle and thoroughbred horses under the canopy of an expansive blue sky.

The road continued its scenic, serpentine upward progress toward the ultimate goal of Prescott—Arizona's first Territorial

The Irascible Cherry Bomb

Capital and Mile High City. (Pronounced locally as Press-cut and not Pres-scot) Once in town, we had a routine of stopping for *essentials* that would get us through the weekend of primitive living. Mom would buy white gas for the stove, a block of ice for the literal icebox, and some kerosene for the lamps. None of us questioned this Thoreau-like existence, as we liked it. If my brothers and I had been perfect on the drive up, Mom would stop at the *Spudnut* shop and buy us a dozen donuts as a treat!

Finally, we would make our way out to our little secluded paradise and happily acknowledge that the old wooden cabin was still standing. Our arrival meant hauling the ice and all the other supplies up the path to the house. Dad or Mom would often buy watermelons and cantaloupes, which on the surface sounds like a normal weekend behavior. However, this meant we would have to store these fruits in the scariest place on the planet, *the cellar!* The cellar was located under the cabin and was open to all

Our cabin in the late 1930s.

creepy living creatures to enter. When Mom or Dad chose me to deliver the melons to this environment, I would holler, stomp my feet on the ground, and clap my hands to make sure that all the vermin and snakes had time to escape before I entered this dark, cool space. Upon arrival, Mom pursued dusting the "mouse dirt" off the beds and furniture, sweeping the floors, shaking out the rugs, washing all flat surfaces, and generally taking control of a building that had been under the supreme command of kangaroo rats and mice since our last visit. Poor Mom! At that time, the world and my family did not know about Hantavirus. I am convinced—but have no scientific proof—we have developed super immunity to these deadly microorganisms since living in this environment for years without any ill health effects.

While Mom was working on sanitizing the interior, my brothers and I had another challenging task. We had to go down to the well—which my father and older brothers had built—to fetch two full water pails. The real test was to carry the two water buckets fifty yards up the hill and arrive in the kitchen with most of the contents still in the pails. My skinny little arms would tremor afterward from the exertion.

After my saintly mother had cleaned the cabin to her standards, she would stand over the hot, white-gas stove cooking dinner for her hungry family. And if we were lucky, it was *tacos* that Mom made extra delicious by adding chorizo to the ground beef and then frying them to a crispy finish. By meal end, your dinner plate was a sea of orange grease.

With dinner over, the best part of the day was sitting in the living room without the benefit of TV or radio. If the night was chilly, we would gather in front of a crackling fire. Our only entertainment source was communication with one another, and with today's world of electronically saturated lifestyles, that would be impossible to imagine. Dad would be seated in his old oak rocking chair while challenging us with brain twisters and often related stories of his early years in Arizona. Mom was always working on crochet handcraft but would add her comments to the subjects discussed. In hindsight, it was an enjoyable experience that unified our nuclear family.

Finally, it would be bedtime. Naturally, we would all have to use the outhouse, which featured a two-person platform and was affectionately called the *pink powder room*. I remember how mortified Peggy—my former wife—was the first time she had to share the double-seater with her future mother-in-law. Why my father thought that was an important feature when he built this privy, I have no clue, but it was another reality of our private paradise we didn't question. During my nightly visits, I remember being scared that some bear or mountain lion would jump out of the darkness and attack me. I carried a flashlight and kept shining the light towards every sound that I imagined I heard. My bigger brother, Ron, seized this opportunity to instill more fear by pointing out obscured shapes in the shadows. During these times, I practiced the 100-yard dash to and fro. Still, I remember the profound silence, the pathway lit by a luminous moon, the immense silver starlight, and the wind whooshing through the towering pine trees—an experience seared in my memory forever.

Those endless summers of my youth seemed to go on and on, filled with extended family get-togethers. When I conjure up memories of those past days, I invariably smile and feel a sense of nostalgia. On the big weekends like Memorial Day, Fourth of July, and Labor Day, many assorted relatives joined the festivities.

During the day, we had an array of activities to entertain us. The most common group activity was long walks through the forest to the natural springs or the railroad tracks. We would collect pottery shards from the ancient original inhabitants, interesting rocks, or rusting railroad spikes along the way. Leonard, Rex, and Ron, my three older brothers, would practice marksmanship with their 22 caliber rifles. We would have multi-generational softball games in the flat area across the creek. A permanent horseshoe court on the north side of the barn featured real horse and mule shoes instead of store-bought ones. It seemed there was always a group surrounding the pits hollering when someone made a ringer. Our Uncle Dale, Dad's brother, was the family champ, as he was a former professional horseshoe player.

I had a few young cousins near my age—Truman, Linda, Glenn— who visited and made the weekends even more fun. And for us kids, we could always find fun things to do: splash in the creek, race homemade boats down the shallow stream, explore the old outbuildings, impromptu prickly pinecone fights, and climb the granite boulders. But at night, the entire extended family would gather around a massive bonfire of raked-up pine needles, pinecones, and gathered wood to talk and roast marshmallows or eat cold slices of watermelon retrieved from *the cellar*. In retrospect, the biggest miracle of these bonfires was that the sparks didn't ignite the bone-dry forest. *Now that would have been memorable!* After all the fresh air and activities, bedtime was a welcome respite.

As I grew up and started inviting friends to spend the weekends with me, I became more conscious of our cabin's shabbiness. It began to appear more like an Appalachian shack than a rustic Arizona summer home. Maybe my friends didn't mind the cracked and broken linoleum floors, the multi-layers of wallpaper all in various stages of peeling, and the soot-covered ceilings that looked like grey velvet. But I did and was embarrassed by these flaws. By this time, the country was going through its 1960s *modern* renaissance. Our little cabin was more a part of the Depression than a part of the Mod '60s. I am sure that I was vocal in my criticism, and maybe others were as well. In August 1964, my father "volunteered" my best friend, Ed Berberian, and me to *remodel* the cabin interior.

Ed was the natural choice to assist me since we had become best friends during high school, and we were almost inseparable. It was evident that neither Ed nor I had any construction experience or even a basic knowledge of how to accomplish this remodel. What we lacked in expertise we made up for in thrift. We were free labor! My other brothers were all married and had lives of their own, so this responsibility fell squarely on my shoulders by default. Of course, Ed and I thought this was a great way to escape Phoenix and the summer heat for a month. Neither of us was concerned about living alone in this isolated abode, cooking our meals, washing our clothes, and doing manual labor that neither of us knew how to complete. It would be an adventure!

The first weekend, Dad opened an account at the local lumber yard where Ed and I could get supplies. We did have transportation, a vintage '49 Chevrolet previously owned by Ed's grandmother, that we used to haul those supplies to the cabin. I think Dad showed us the basics of how to hang sheetrock, tape it, texture it, and then sand it. Okay, we could do that! First, we had to remove the old fiberboard that had held the walls together for many decades. Like archeologists, we discovered the pack rats had made those walls home and included many new artifacts like cactus thorns, stuffing from the cabin's furniture, and pinecones. After removal and cleaning, we would hang the sheetrock and go through all the steps until we would ultimately paint the rooms. It was a lot of work and took more time than we anticipated. The final result was better than when we started but was far from a professional job. What could anyone expect from two untrained high school students more interested in fine arts than in manual arts?

By 21st century standards, the rare parents would allow two high school teenagers to hang out at a cabin unsupervised for a month. But once again, it was a different time, and Ed and I were good kids. Our daily tasks kept us busy and out of trouble. Feeling like modern-day pioneers, we had to wash our clothes and bodies in a large galvanized tub with water hauled up the hill from the well. We had to buy our food and cook it on the old white gas stove. And we were both surprised that the icebox managed to keep the perishable food amazingly cold. Our only link to the outside world was a transistor radio and the one Prescott station, KNOT. A couple of Sundays, we went into town to church and MYF--Methodist Youth Fellowship--in a vain attempt to make friends with some locals.

The highlight of our month-long solitude was when some of our high school friends--June Masters, Gene Mayer, Sharlee Franklin, and Harry Dean--came for a weekend visit along with my parents. Saturday night, the six of us packed into Ed's old Chevy and drove into town to the Senator Drive-In to see an unmemorable movie. Being teenage *sophisticates* from the big city, we laughed at this mini-version of a drive-in compared to Phoenix's much larger and more luxurious drive-ins. *Hello! A drive-in is a drive-in!* Another weekend Uncle Dale and Aunt Adelaide showed up for a surprise visit and Sunday BBQ. It was a great visit and is tucked away in my memory as it was the last time Uncle Dale would be able to do such an outing. He passed away that Thanksgiving from brain cancer.

Every story has an ending, and our exclusive paradise story ended due to the US Forest Service bureaucracy. After my father passed away in 1969, it ended his 99-year lease with the government. It took three years before the Forest Service contacted us and said that we had to return the property to its natural state. Of course, the family tried to fight the ruling, but we demolished and removed all buildings in the end. The lush forest and isolated dell still exist, and I visit it often in my dreams and occasionally in real life. But the memories will live on as long as I do. And the special place that I have selected to have my ashes scattered is next to that perennial creek of my youth—in my personal paradise.

Wayne H. Brewster

All of these photos are from the late 1940s.

The Irascible Cherry Bomb

WAYNE H. BREWSTER

2020

Labels Suck!

We all carry labels, and sometimes the toting sucks!
Hi, I'm Wayne, and I'm a label-aholic. I'm an Aries, male, white, senior-citizen, gay, American now expatriate, born Glendalian and Arizonan, Baby Boomer, Sun Devil, Democrat, formerly Methodist, and now an omnist. Whew! That's a lengthy label list to own and wear. Please don't call me a WASP, although I could belong to the *Daughters of the American Revolution* if I were female. I've long moved past that limiting marker.

Growing up in the mid-twentieth century, everyone carried labels. Most of us still do. I detest them. I've never felt the harsh stigma of prejudice, as I grew up under white male privilege. Oh, I've had brushes with it during my lifetime. During my college years at Arizona State University, I joined Zeta Beta Tau, a Jewish fraternity, and married a Catholic. A few of my narrow-minded relatives thought I had lost it and voiced their opinions on my choices. Boy, they're turning over in their graves now since I also carry the gay label. Whatever! Speaking of my sexuality, I had a non-binary friend who, once I came out, always introduced me as their "gay-friend Wayne." Geez, I didn't present this person as my heterosexual friend. See what I mean? Friggin' labels. They're annoying, and we need to move past them as a society.

A news article I recently read provoked me to express my feelings regarding labels and their prejudicial nature. It seems certain people are applying pressure on a leading national specialty grocer to change some of their packaging that, while creative, could be remotely interpreted as racist. Examples included the label *José* on imported Mexican beer, *Ming* on some frozen Asian foods, and *Giotto* on Italian specialties. Now, I think that is ridiculous and going too far towards political correctness. Is our country going to force all Josés to change their name to Joe? It is only a name that has ethnic origins and doesn't signify racism in the slightest. Let's address pressing issues and not get caught up in trivial pursuit.

I'm reasonably sure most of you have been shocked and dismayed over the open racism in the United States recently. I know I am. When Obama got elected to office, I sighed with relief, thinking that this country had finally moved forward and left denoting a person's skin color in the past. I should have seen the warning signs with the nasty comments made during his presidency. Then it looked as if America was ready to elect a female president. As I watched the election results, that hopeful breakthrough crashed and burned. The next four years saw every hatred and prejudice surface and flourished again. One might call it an emotional and intellectual civil war. I've never understood humanity and its divisions based on skin color, sex, religion, or ethnicity. Change and acceptance need to happen now!

The Irascible Cherry Bomb

WE are all one people with common goals. We've got to stop labeling people and hating them for their differences. We must work together to change this situation and end racism, sexism, and labeling.

2016

March in Morelia

For the past several weeks, our city has transformed itself from its dowdy brown winter jacket into a frilly multi-floral frock. The deciduous trees are all sporting fresh lime-green leaves, and hundreds of azalea shrubs have burst into bloom in varying shades of pink, red, lavender, yellow, and white. Thanks to the increased sunshine and temperate weather, the bougainvillea are masses of vibrant color, almost too brilliant to view.

But the most spectacular spring show is reserved for the jacarandas. Thankfully, these South American-native trees grow everywhere in Morelia, which has created a temporary streetscape similar to a Mardi Gras parade. Large lavender poufs dot the city and line the main thoroughfares. The trees' branches bend from their purple plumes' weight, which, in-turn, litters the streets with lavender floral confetti, like the aftermath of the famous carnival. And when the cars pass on the road, these spent blossoms flutter in the air like exotic butterflies, only to return to the pavement for the next blast of air to carry them upward. Our mild climate will allow a steady progression of other trees to bloom, which will change the palette of the cityscape from purple to yellow to orange creating a natural floral rainbow.

2020

Places of Plenitude

What do Arizona's Valley of the Sun *(Phoenix, Glendale, Mesa, Tempe)*, San Francisco, and Morelia have in common? They are all fantastic places that I've been lucky enough to call home. Each area is exceptional, like apples, oranges, and bananas in a big ol' fruit bowl. Still, the common denominator is that they provided me with the necessary ingredients for a long, and dare I say, fruitful life.

I suppose I will always call Arizona home. It holds the longest and deepest roots. My foundation. My family. My comfort zone. I still insist on visiting it at least twice a year to maintain long-term friendships, to be with my family, and for the abundant shopping and dining opportunities. Yet, it has changed significantly over the decades, and not always for the better. Gone are the endless citrus groves, lush grape vineyards, fertile farm fields, and the shady oasis-like towns, all surrounded by pristine desert. Looking back, I either took this paradise for granted or didn't recognize its uniqueness. Progress and population have replaced this Garden of Eden with a sprawling tiled-roof, freeway-laced, urban center mirroring southern California. But here and there exist glimpses of old Arizona. My Arizona. It's only a long drive to find it.

During those early years of residency, the Phoenix area offered little in the way of food diversity. Of course, we had abundant Mexican and Chinese food cafes to supplement the meatloaf and mashed potato banality. Another exception, since 1949, Miracle Mile Deli was offering the best of Jewish deli food, and I ate there at least once a week when I worked at Park Central's Goldwaters. I remember discovering Phoenix's first Italian bakery on Seventh Avenue in the 1970s, which was a real treat to have crusty fragrant loaves for our home dinner parties. People went gaga when Duck and Decanter opened in 1972, as they were the first gourmet kitchen store in town, also serving the most delectable brown-bagged sandwiches. Then C. Steele & Co. opened in Scottsdale with a French flair in culinary necessities and delicious café fare. Little by little, Phoenix developed a broader culinary diversity.

The year 1969 was one of those years in my life where I can look back in amazement at all that happened. Men landed on the moon. Woodstock. Charles Manson. Chappaquiddick. Boeing 747 debuted. I completed my senior year and second year as editor in chief of ASU's Sahuaro yearbook. I married Peggy Curran, and we moved to San Francisco. It was a delightful escape from white-bread Phoenix to embrace a crusty-sourdough cosmopolitan city.

Three years of newlywed bliss and discovery entailed a life very similar to the famous book and television series *Tales of the City*. Hell, we even lived in the same Russian Hill neighborhood as Anna Madrigal's Barbary Lane fictional residence.

WAYNE H. BREWSTER

On our Union and Hyde corner stood the original Swensen's Ice Cream parlor, Marcel et Henri Charcuterie, and Searchlight Market, three famous San Francisco institutions. I would often ride the Hyde Street cable car to my job at the old Emporium Department Store on Market Street. Of course, like all the other young wannabe hipsters, we did our weekly shopping at the Marina Safeway store, famous for its hetro hookups and extensive wine selection. We binged on Irish coffees at The Buena Vista, and I have to report it's a mean drunk. All that caffeine, Irish whiskey, whipped cream, and sugar make for a rough night. We learned all the different Chinese cuisines while picking up a few basic Cantonese phrases. We ate our fill of Dungeness crab and discerned which sourdough bakery was the best. We ate cannoli in Little Italy, washed down with an espresso. We explored northern California with passionate zeal and learned the difference between Cabernet Sauvignon and Zinfandel wine. It was heaven! It was the ideal learning experience for two naïve kids on their own for the first time. It ended when we returned to Phoenix to raise a family, live closer to our mutual families, and give me a new job opportunity. Peg and I still look back and consider those very magical times in our lives.

I must relate a true story concerning Peg. When we were dating, she would often bring me brownies that were simply the best. After moving to San Francisco, I came home from work one day and could smell the brownies when I entered our apartment. Naturally, I was thrilled and had to have a small square even before dinner. I took a bite and then another one and said in my most undiplomatic voice, "Something is seriously wrong with this batch. They don't remotely taste the same as the ones you use to bake in Phoenix." She looked me in the eye and sheepishly stated, "I never baked those. My mother did." Dumfounded, I squeaked, "What? I married you for those brownies, and now you tell me they were your mother's? I should have married her!" Luckily, I didn't divorce her right then and there, but Peg eventually turned into an excellent home baker and cook for someone without necessary kitchen skills.

I now call Morelia home. It is a world heritage city full of culture, a mild climate, beautiful architectural treasures, and a wonderful place to live or to visit. Off the radar to most of my fellow countrymen, it is hard to convince them of the beauty and quality of life found here. The local cuisine has a UNESCO world heritage designation. Based on indigenous recipes, the food is like nothing else in the world. It falls under the category of Mexican food but defies comparison. For example, uchepos and corundas are local tamales but not like their meat-filled northern cousins. Sopa Tarasca is a bean and tomato-based, thick soup, which is one of my favorite dishes. Slightly spicy, it also has a smokey quality to it. Probably the most famous food is carnitas, twice-cooked pork. You haven't lived until you wrap a warm tortilla around this succulent meat garnished with salsa, cilantro, chopped onions, and a dab of guacamole. Talk about heaven in one bite. I must admit that I've tried the local dessert called chongos. It must be an acquired taste; as for me, it is repulsive. Imagine big chunks of curdled milk floating in a sweetened caramelized sauce. Oh, yum. Naturally, Morelia is a modern city too. We have a wide variety of delightful restaurants and different cuisines to enjoy. I hate to admit it, but the city is also full of U.S. chains, like Burger King, Carls Jr., Chili's, IHOP, McDonald's, KFC, Little Ceasar,

Dominos, Subway, and that list goes on to end in dietary boredom. You can't escape them. Despite the plethora of universal fast food and big-box stores, it is a magical place to live.

People have asked me if I could live anywhere in the world, where would I choose? One word: Italy. More specifically, Florence. My first visit there was in February 1978. It was a business trip for Goldwaters Department Stores, and I accompanied Miss Mary Newell, our gift buyer. She had visited several times previously and knew the lay of the land. But for me, it was all new and a revelation. Never had I walked in such history nor eaten such delicious food. I became a fan of everything Italian after that first trip.

I must tell you a funny story about Miss Newell. Our Florence office had a home store specialist, Lisa Lentucci, who would schedule our factory visits based on our product input. Each day, we would climb into a big Mercedes and head out into the country to visit specific factories. Our company-hired driver was a very handsome man named Sergio. Well, our Miss Newell was single and quite taken with this man. Mary and I sat in the backseat, and she was always telling me how handsome he was and how she would love to get to know him better, "if you know what I mean." It was all safe and innocent chatter because we spoke in English, and Sergio only spoke Italian. Daily, after many hours of factory visits, we would stop for a long lunch at various local restaurants with exquisite food. This one particular day, Lisa excused herself to freshen up in the washroom. Not being fluent in Italian, Mary and I relied on Lisa to translate the menus for us. Mary and I discussed the list and wished out loud that Lisa could translate it for us. Suddenly, Sergio spoke up in perfect English that he could explain the menu to us. Miss Newell almost fainted and slid under the table with embarrassment, but I, on the other hand, couldn't stop laughing. All her lusting and suggestive comments he clearly understood, and he was professional enough not to respond. There were so many memorable funny stories on that trip that I shall remember to the day I die. Unfortunately, most of them involve Mary's mishaps, and she may not recognize them as being so funny.

Over the next four years, I had the good fortune to visit Florence twice a year for a week at a time. During those visits, I grew to adore northern Italian food. To this day, it is my favorite cuisine, and I learned to cook many of their specialties. On that first trip, Miss Newell introduced me to this rustic restaurant called *Trattoria Sostanza*. It became my favorite place to eat, and it still exists today and has been feeding the public since 1869. I remember thinking that some of the waiters had been there since they opened, and they were borderline rude in dealing with their customers. "Tell me what you want, and we'll bring it to you," that sort of attitude. However, people keep coming back time after time for their Florentine steak and chicken breast fried in butter. It's that damn chicken breast that was love at first bite, and I had to perfect that recipe for home cooking. Over the years, I've served it a hundred times, at least. People rave over it.

So I've written this entire dissertation so I could present you with my recipe. I hope wandering through all my words was worth the final goal. Try it! I know you'll like it! *Buon appetito!*

Wayne H. Brewster

Italian Fried Chicken *(Petti de Pollo al Burro)*

One of my standard and favorite recipes to fix for family and friends. Serves: 4.

4 boneless skinless chicken breast halves

½ cup flour

¼ cup finely grated Parmesan cheese

2 sticks butter

¼ cup olive oil

Salt and pepper to taste

¼ cup minced fresh parsley (optional)

1 – 2 lemons (juiced)

Pound the chicken breasts with a meat mallet, rolling pin, or heavy skillet to half their original thickness (about 1/4-inch thick). In a large frying pan over medium heat, melt one stick of butter and the olive oil. Mix the flour and parmesan cheese in a bowl. Once the oil mixture has reached medium heat, dip the chicken breasts in the flour/Parmesan cheese mixture and shake off the excess. If necessary, add to the pan in batches so as not to crowd the breasts. Salt and pepper the chicken. Fry the chicken breasts turning once until golden brown, approximately 10 to 15 minutes. Remove the breasts to a warm platter. Turn up the heat under the skillet to medium-high. Add the new stick of butter and melt completely; add the lemon juice. With a spoon, scrape up the browned bits and deglaze the pan; cook for 15 to 20 seconds to slightly thicken. At this point, you may add the optional parsley and swiftly incorporate it into the sauce. Adjust salt and pepper to taste. Pour the sauce over the chicken on the platter and serve immediately. You may want to garnish the plate with additional lemon slices or parsley sprigs.

2021

Horsefeathers!

Last week, I stumbled upon Netflix's *History of Swear Words*, and I quickly learned it's not for an old *Goody-Two-Shoes* like me. Watching several episodes, I became numb to certain swear words' incessant usage, and the dialog grew tiresome and offensive. Damn it!

I'm not proud to say that I use swear words in my daily conversations. Who would believe that I was born into a family that never, ever used profanity? My parents were righteous, stalwart people, and never uttered a swear word in their lives. They expected and demanded the same of my brothers and me. I remember getting my mouth washed out with soap, but I can't remember for what violation. Surely, not for cursing, as I would be dead now. I think it was my college years before I picked up the habit of swearing, along with smoking and drinking. Being cool required it. Shit, man, it was the 60s.

I've given up trying to be cool as it's too much work. I gave up smoking seven years ago and rarely drink and never to excess. Maybe the timing is right to give up cussing.

Wayne H. Brewster

During my youth, there existed clean swearwords that one would use in place of offensive language. My youthful role model was my cousin Truman Brewster. His family had the same high standards of no profanity, but he had some of the most inventive ways to insert colorful, clean cursing into his speech. His holy trinity of cuss words was *horsepucky, bullpucky,* and *bull crap.* I was more prone to use *shoot, son of a gun,* and *golly.* And we never uttered these words in earshot of our parents.

I think it's time that the world returns to the kinder, less-inflammatory, Wonder-Bread communication style of the mid-twentieth century. Of course, sans racial, gender, and sexual orientation epithets. We can start by switching out contemporary cuss words for cleaner versions.

- How about *dadgummit?* It sort of rolls off the tongue and conveys a certain *je ne sais quoi* and sounds more sophisticated than *dagnabbit.*
- *Holy cow! Holy succotash! Holy guacamole! Heavens to Betsy! Hell's bells!* All of these allow us to tread lightly on religious pedigrees without provoking the Lord's name in vain.
- *Sugar!* It's just too sweet to catch on. But if you use the word in conjunction with several others, it becomes significant: *Sugar Honey Ice Tea.*
- Some variations on the same theme above are *Crud. Crap. Crapola. Phooey. Poo on a stick.* I don't know about you, but they don't sit well on my tongue.
- *Shucks. Darn. Gosh darnit. Heck. Drat. Oh my gosh! Gee whiz.* They are of the Hubert Humphrey school of cussing and are perfectly safe.

The Irascible Cherry Bomb

- Southerners talk funny and can entertain a crowd with their colloquialisms. I'm very fond of their *"Bless his/her heart"* phrase, which translates to *"the bitch is bat shit crazy!"* A few more southern expressions: *What the heck? What on earth? H. E. Double LL. Son of a bee sting. Horsefeathers. Shut the front door!* Make sure to deliver them with a convincing drawl.
- I like *leapin' lizards*. Perfect for those of you named Annie.
- *Geez Louise*. I use it a lot in my writing, so I'll keep that one.
- *Great Scott! Jiminy Cricket! Holy schnikes!* They're too old-school Hollywood for me, but use them if you want.

I can't think of any more clean cuss words, but if you think I should keep racking my brain on this subject, just f*&# off!

2012

Feast Day of Guadalupe

December 12 is one of the most important days of the Mexican calendar. It's the holy day of the Virgin of Guadalupe, also known as *Our Lady of Guadalupe, Patroness of Americas, Empress of Latin American, and Queen of Mexico*. All of which signifies this icon of the Virgin Mary.

This year we are celebrating the 480th anniversary of her apparition to Saint Juan Diego[1] . As the story goes, on December 9, 1531, the Virgin appeared to the peasant, Juan Diego, in the Tepeyac desert near Mexico City. In speaking with Juan Diego, the Virgin requested his help in building a church in her name where they were standing. Juan Diego—of Aztec descent but a recent convert to Christianity—rushed to Bishop Juan De Zumárraga to tell him of the sighting and the Virgin's request. First, however, the Bishop requested more proof of her appearance.

---

1. Juan Diego was named a saint by Pope John Paul II in 1990 at the Basilica of Guadalupe in Mexico City. His saint day is celebrated on December 9th.

The Irascible Cherry Bomb

Juan Diego returned to the same place each day, waiting for her second appearance. Finally, on December 12, the Virgin returned, and Juan Diego told her of the Bishop's request. She instructed Juan Diego to climb the Tepeyac Hill, where he would find Castilian roses blooming. He did indeed climb the hill and saw the specified roses, which remarkably were the same type found in the Bishop's Spanish hometown and would not be blooming in December. Juan Diego gathered the roses in his cape and took them to the Bishop to prove the Virgin's sighting. Upon opening his cloak to show the Bishop the roses, images of the roses and the Virgin miraculously appeared on the cape's interior.

Today you can see Saint Juan Diego's actual cape on display in the Basilica of Guadalupe on the site of the first sighting. It's suspended over the altar of the basilica and preserved in a large glass box.

The Virgin of Guadalupe became intertwined with the Mexican Independence through the *"Grito"* of Hidalgo—when Don Miguel Hidalgo y Costilla called the peasants to rise against the tyranny of the Spaniards—shouting the now-famous "¡Viva México! ¡Viva la Virgen de Guadalupe!" Over the last two hundred years, her symbol has become ingrained in this country's most basic fiber. Hence, masses and fiestas commemorate her day in churches, hospitals, private schools, businesses, and public spaces. It's not an official government celebration but a public celebration of devotion to the Catholic Church and faith in general.

Once, I visited the epicenter of Morelia's celebration, Templo San Diego, one of my favorite churches in Morelia. It showcases beyond-exuberant decorations—gold-leafed, bas-relief plaster architectural features; hot pink walls; borders of 3-D gigantic realistically painted plaster flowers; and a substantial gilt-framed image of the Virgin of Guadalupe hanging above the altar. Upon entering the sanctuary, the visuals overwhelm you with part baroque, part Mexican-style, and part Hollywood theatrics, but somehow as a whole, it seems to work in inspiring. I wanted to enter the church on this feast night, but it would have been a very long wait. Thousands lined up to gain entry and show their devotion to the Virgin. But I was able to get close enough to the open main doors to peer inside. The already over-decorated sanctuary looked even more opulent, with banks of pink roses gracing the walls and altar. At the same time, the immense crystal chandeliers glistened brightly over the surging devoted crowd. A sizeable Mexican flag was draped artistically beneath the framed Virgin image, symbolizing the Virgin unifying Catholicism and the Republic forever.

Outside the temple, it was chaos. All the surrounding streets were closed, and row after row of stalls occupied the space. Vendors were selling videos, jewelry, clothing, food, and every item imaginable in a carnival atmosphere. But the most common concessions seemed to be sugar cane chunks and roasted peanuts. Of the five hundred stalls existing within the church's many blocks, I would estimate that one-hundred-plus stalls were selling these two items. I don't know what that says about the attendees' tastes, but where were the corn dogs, cotton candy, funnel cakes, and turkey drumsticks of our state fairs? Maybe I need to introduce the Mexicans to real festival foods!

But the most lasting impression of that night was walking down the Calzada—a broad pedestrian walkway—that leads directly to the church. The faithful made their way to the temple, dressed in indigenous costumes, and carrying lighted candles or bouquets of roses. The most pious pilgrims were crawling on their knees as family members relayed blankets from the back to the front of the person crawling to protect their knees from the rigid cobble-stoned walkway.

Outlying pueblo churches rented buses to bring parishioners to the celebration. These devoted people came in Purépecha colorful native dress with a brass band and banners—emblazoned with the Virgin's image—announcing the town. Each group choreographed dances and swayed their way down the Calzada. Their wooden sandals slapped on the stones created a rhythmic accompaniment to the band's notes. These scenes brought me to tears at the spectacle, beauty, and sincerity exhibited. However, I did laugh at the irony of one dancer in traditional native garb taking out his cell phone and having a conversation while being part of a centuries-old dance. It spoke eloquently of Mexico's two repeatedly colliding worlds of ancient and modern.

I drove home contented, having witnessed an integral part of Mexico's love of traditions and fiestas.

2013

Latkes

It's December, and there is finally a little chill in the air in central Mexico. Regardless of where I'm living—Phoenix or Morelia—when the weather cools down, I instantly want to change my meal planning to more seasonally appropriate foods.

One of my favorite meals this time of year is in celebration of Hanukkah. Tonight is the last night of this week-long celebration, so what could be better than a savory brisket with traditional latkes on the side? Okay, forget the brisket, but give me those crisp, golden-brown potato pancakes. *I love latkes!!!* What's not to love?

This recipe that I've included below is certified delicious, although not strictly kosher. (Add matzo meal instead of flour, and then it's kosher.) I have used it for years. But now the controversy begins; do you prefer your latkes garnished with sour cream or applesauce? I love them with the sweet and seasonally appropriate applesauce. But I'll let your taste buds be your guide.

So tonight, I will be making these wonderful lacy pancakes and celebrating the season of light. Happy Hanukkah! Shalom!

Kartoffel Pfannkuchen (German Potato Pancakes)

Christie Williams wrote the first-ever Cuisinart food processor cookbook in 1979, and this recipe is from that book. You may serve them with sour cream or applesauce on the side. Serves: 6.

2 tablespoons fresh parsley, chopped

1 small onion, chopped

2 eggs

2 tablespoons flour or matzo meal

1 ½ teaspoons salt

½ teaspoon white pepper

2 teaspoons freshly grated nutmeg

6 medium potatoes, peeled

1 cup butter

If you don't own a food processor, substitute hand techniques using a knife and metal grater. In the processor bowl fitted with the steel knife, mince the parsley and set it aside. Cut the onion into quarters and process using the steel knife by pulsing until finely chopped. Add the eggs, parsley, flour, and spices to the onion in the processor bowl and briefly blend. Remove the steel knife and inset the shredding disc on its stem. Grate the potatoes into the onion/egg mixture. Remove the shredding disc and stir to combine the potatoes with the egg mixture. Heat the butter to 1/4-inch deep in a heavy skillet over medium heat. Drop 1/3-cup of the potato mixture for each pancake into the skillet. Flatten the pancakes out with a spatula until they are 1/2-inch thick. It is usually possible to do four pancakes at a time. When the pancakes are golden brown on one side, turn and cook until crisp and brown on the other side. Be sure to allow plenty of time, as it takes a while for them to cook through. Adjust the heat as required and add more butter if necessary. Remove the cooked pancakes to paper towels on a baking sheet and keep warm in the oven while frying the remainder. Transfer to a warm platter and serve.

(Please note: You will notice that the pancake batter tends to become rather juicy as it sits. Do not stir this liquid back into the mixture, but instead drain the excess off and discard.)

2019

European Christmas Vacation

"We're all gonna have so much fun we're gonna need plastic surgery to remove our smiles!"

Who said that? Clark Griswold initially, but I made it my mantra. With the same unbridled optimism, I organized a 1988 Christmas vacation to Germany and Austria for my family. On the journey with me were my wife Peg, our two teenage children Lauren and John, Peg's 71-year-old mother Marge, and Marge's best friend Dorothy, who was comparable to the dingy aunt every family has. I mean, what could go wrong on a two-week Christmas family vacation to Europe?

With all my exact time and action planning, I visualized a storybook Germanic Christmas of white glistening snow, horse-drawn sleigh rides, ski lessons for the kids, ice skating, famous Christkindlesmarkt visits, charming countryside excursions, Silent Night sung by angelic children, warm woolen mittens, grilled bratwursts, and fragrant fir-filled rooms everywhere. We would visit Munich, Nuremberg, Salzburg, and hunker-down for almost a week in Oberammergau, Bavaria. Perfect. Even Rick Steves couldn't plan an itinerary as good as mine. No doubts crossed my mind about six people in two cars traveling through Europe with only a road map to guide us and with me being the only semi-German-speaking person. Exuding confidence, I said, "It'll be fine." In retrospect, I was obscenely naive.

After a day flying from Phoenix to Munich via New York City, we landed in a snowstorm. I said, "Look, kids! We're going to have a white Christmas!"

Peg replied, "Yes, and we're going to be driving in it." In most of these situations, she tended to be the clanking-snow-chains on the tires of life.

We would be driving two rented cars to carry all the luggage and family comfortably. When I reserved them, it never occurred to me that Peg had never driven a stickshift. Well, no problem! I decided she could master it quickly. So I gave her driving lessons in the parking lot, while her mother stood there glaring at me, bundled up in a hooded coat like Obi-Wan Kenobi, and watching her mouth move. I'm sure she wished that the Force was with me. After fifteen-minutes of Peg's protests and tears and with Marge cursing me, Peg and I returned to the rental counter to exchange the offending car for one with an automatic transmission. The female agent, decked out in her tailored military-ish uniform, was dumbfounded and tried to reason with us, "Du vant an automatic? Da standard ist mas schön fur de snow und ice! Unbelievable, you Americans!" I looked the agent in the eye and said through gritted teeth, "You don't understand. The Cold War was nothing compared to what I have suffered through this morning. Just give us a damn automatic transmission car so we can be on our way."

The Irascible Cherry Bomb

This exchange did nothing to enhance our German-American relationships.

We finally left the airport in our separate cars, headed for our hotel in central Munich, located strategically across from the Oktoberfest park. I took the lead with John and Marge riding with me. Peg and Lauren were in the other car. Exiting the airport for the autobahn to the city, I went through a yellow stoplight, which Peg didn't get through. I stopped my vehicle approximately fifty meters ahead on the access road's shoulder to let Peg catch up. We waited and waited and waited and no Peg! I reasoned she had taken the other exit at the stoplight, and I said calmly, "She'll find her way."

Well, this put my mother-in-law into an over-the-edge, hand-wringing panic mode and begging me to do something. "What do you want me to do about it? She'll discover her mistake eventually."

Remember, this tense exchange occurred in the days well before cellphones and GPS. You had to rely on maps, an innate sense of direction, and the kindness of strangers to help you find your way.

Peg and Lauren were on their way towards Czechlosvakia and clueless as to where they were going. After traveling a few dozen kilometers in the wrong direction, Peg stopped at a service station. Not speaking German, she pointed in the direction she was headed and asked, "Munich?" She received a response from several shaking heads and with them pointing in the opposite direction. So armed with this valuable knowledge, Peg and Lauren started back towards Munich. The situation wasn't entirely hopeless, as they did have the hotel's address and a map. Unfortunately, this was useless as they couldn't understand the streets' jumble and the unpronounceable German names. Desperate and near tears, Peg and Lauren were fighting with the street map, trying to determine where they were and how to get to where they were going. Finally, two young men in a car next to them saw that they were lost and upset and motioned for Peg to roll down her window. Sensing them to be saviors, Peg yelled to them the name and address of the hotel. They nodded and motioned for Peg to follow them.

Lauren screamed, "You're not going to follow them, are you?"

Peg scolded, "Your father abandoned us, and we have no other choice. We're following them."

Being good Samaritans, they led Peg and Lauren to the hotel, where we were waiting with faces pressed up against the glass for their arrival. As expected, I received the blame for Peg's wrong turn and have the back-lashing scars to prove it.

This day was only the first of fourteen! Thank you, Clark Griswold. You idiot!

On the second day, Peg and I drove back to the airport to fetch Dorothy, our crazy pseudo-aunt, who at the time lived in El Paso, Texas, and worked as a nursing school professor at UTEP. Self-righteously, I drove and didn't get lost going or returning to the hotel since I have a perfect innate sense of direction. While Dorothy unpacked and rested from jetlag, I consulted the time and action plan and noted we should visit the Christkindlesmarkt downtown. Our family unit of five took the subway from the Goetheplatz station two-stops to Marienplatz, our destination. What a joy to tour the holiday market and try all the traditional foods—warm waffles *mit Schlag* (whipped cream), sugar and spice-glazed almonds, hot mulled wine, and grilled savory bratwursts. We also bought beautiful traditional ornaments to hang on our forthcoming *Tannenbaum*. Ahh, my dream was coming true. After many hours exploring Munich's historical center and the fair, we decided to head back to the hotel for a nap. Entering the subway or U-Bahn, we all jumped on the long, steep escalator descending to the station. I was in front with Peg, John, Lauren, and Marge following stair-stepped behind me like ducks in a row.

Being the week before Christmas, it was beyond crowded and chaotic. It seemed manic, and I urged everyone to stay close. Once reaching the bottom, I headed over to the system map to ensure which train to take back to our stop. Once satisfied, I turned around and asked Peg, "Where's your mother?" Lauren says, "She was right behind me on the escalator." Panic set in. I begin running around, searching for Marge. No Marge! I immediately thought someone had kidnapped her, but quickly realized nobody would want her. Bewildered and anxious, Peg and I decided that our only immediate option was to head back to the hotel and have them call the police. Our grave concern intensified with the realization that Marge had no idea where we were staying and was deathly afraid to speak to a German. Losing Grandma put a severe crimp in my time and action family-fun plan.

In my head, I started planning my description of Marge for the police. Short, plump, old, Irish-American, easily excitable, and mean as a snake when provoked. Perhaps Peg could flesh out my sketchy description.

We arrived back at the hotel only to find Marge on her hands and knees, screaming into her room through the door's mail slot,

"Dorothy! Dorothy, wake up. It's me, Marge! Open the door!" She then heard us talking while entering the hallway and slowly stood up to her full four feet, ten inches, and redirected her anger at us, "Why the hell did you leave me?"

All of us began talking in unison, "We didn't. Are you okay? How did you get back to the hotel? Thank God you're here! We were so worried."

She sighed in disgust and explained, "Well, I thought you all ran ahead and jumped on the train and left me. I was furious, but I waited and caught the next train. I went to the second stop and got off. When I came up to the street level, I knew this was our neighborhood as I spotted some stores that I had seen last night when we walked to dinner. So then I went back to the hotel, and I discovered that you weren't here. I've been banging on this door and yelling for ten minutes, trying to get into my room, but Dorothy refuses to let me in. She keeps mumbling, 'Go away! I'm not letting you in!' I guess she thinks I'm housekeeping or something. Maybe she took a sleeping pill as she is out of it."

After our emotions calmed down, I explained how lucky she was to have gotten on the right train since that station connects lines from all over the city. We might not have ever found her. She might have become someone's Haus Frau scrubbing floors and learning to cook *Wienerschnitzel*. I daydreamed about that tempting scenario but once again asked myself, "who would want her?"

After that harrowing experience, I filled out sheets of paper with the name and addresses of where we stayed for everyone to carry with them if we got separated. Every morning during breakfast, I would ask each person if they had the list with them. Live and learn.

The Irascible Cherry Bomb

After Munich, we visited Nuremberg and the oldest and most famous Christkindlesmarkt. Our strategically located hotel overlooked the market's red and white striped awning-covered stalls, and we all sat at our windows, gazing out at this magical scene. In those few precious moments, my happy-family-vacation goals materialized. Here they were chatting away amicably about their experiences of exploring the market while visions of warm cinnamon and sugar-scented almonds danced in my head. It made all the craziness of the last few days worthwhile.

We met some friends for dinner, and they gifted us with a lovely tin of authentic *Lebkuchen* gingerbread cookies, one of Nuremberg's iconic products. The next day, we headed south to Oberammergau, of passion play fame, nestled in the snowy German Alps' foothills. It's a charming Bavarian village with its elaborately painted facades and the perfect place to spend Christmas. We had rented a large apartment for a week, and we would take day trips out to see all the beautiful sights close by—King Ludwig's castles, Wieskirche, Berchtesgaden, and Garmish-Partenkirchen.

After checking in and unpacking, the next business order was to find a fresh Christmas tree for our apartment. We had collected enough ornaments and sweets to decorate our tree, including real candles and their holders. I was determined to find a traditional German Christmas tree to match my visual image. It had to be a luscious fragrant fir with delicate tiered branches in a symmetric pyramidal shape. John and I headed out on our holy mission. We searched the entire town and two other close-by towns. We couldn't find a Christmas tree lot to save our souls. Here we were in Bavaria, the birthplace of Christmas trees, and we couldn't find one. This fact dumbfounded me and made me even more intent on finding one. I finally stopped at a local florist to ask where we might secure a full-sized tree. They said the only place was behind the local church. I never thought to look there! Sure enough, dozens of trees laid covered by snow in a yard behind the parish church. These were all forest-harvested fir trees and not farm-grown groomed ones, so their branches were well-spaced and open-formed. I was in awe! I felt like I had found the Holy Grail of Christmas trees. John seemed a bit less enthusiastic. Ignoring his blasé attitude, I said, "Now, how do we pay for it? "

Nobody was around to ask. So I searched for and found the parish office and explained the situation in my broken German. They indicated that the tree cost the equivalent of 3.50 dollars. Wow, I was ecstatic over the price. I proudly brought the six-foot tree into the apartment for the family to see it, and Peg, the eternal critic, said, "That's the ugliest tree I've ever seen." The rest of the critics broke out into peals of laughter, pointing at me holding my beloved tree.

Trying to cover my hurt feelings, I replied defensively, "This was the best one available as there are hard to find. And it's the cheapest Christmas tree we've ever had." To which Peg replied, "Yes, it only cost you a trip to Europe to find it!" Talk about a bitch slap! Merry Friggin' Christmas to you too.

For all of us on this trip, it remains our best Christmas ever. Annually, we retell this vacation's other stories that are now part of our family lore. The list includes a special Christmas Eve dinner of roasted goose and baked Alaska at Ommeramergau's Hotel Turmwirt and afterward, a magnificent world-class midnight mass in the local church. It featured a full orchestra, a German brass band, and a lovely chorus. We huddled together in the sanctuary's cold and candle-lit interior, listening to the beautiful music. Suddenly, a procession entered carrying the Christchild and placed him in the manger. At that very moment, the crystal chandeliers blazed in a burst of dazzling light while the music crescendoed. It was a dramatic end to a beautiful evening.

The rest of the trip was full of idyllic winter adventures like skiing, sledding, and ice skating. As our itinerary was slowly coming to a close, we head to Austria. We celebrated Marge's December 29th birthday in Salzburg in a candle-lit restaurant, and she even exclaimed it was her best birthday ever. Two days later, on New Year's Eve, we returned to Munich to catch our New Year's Day flight home. At midnight, Peg, the kids, and I huddled together in the nearby Oktoberfest park, where hundreds of people were setting off fireworks. Even though it was a foggy night, the fireworks were like watching a psychedelic light show. Brief bursts of color and light brightened the gloomy cloud-filled sky. It was a celebratory end to two glorious weeks.

The entire family decorated our German Christmas tree in the Oberammergau apartment.

In striking contrast, the next day was a sad and disturbing experience at the Munich airport checking in for our flight. This departure was ten days after the tragic bombing of the Frankfurt-originated Pan Am flight over Lockerbie, Scotland, and German airports were on an ultra-rigid security alert. None of us had experienced machine-gun-toting military men checking our luggage and bodies for any explosives and their repeated questioning. It was unnerving, and our kids were frightened over it.

Even after thirty-plus years, it remains a Griswold family-ish vacation never forgotten.

Nuremberg hotel overlooking the Christkindlesmarkt - John, Wayne, Lauren, and Peggy Brewster

The Irascible Cherry Bomb

Nuremberg's famed Christkindlesmarkt and its Frauenkirche church.

Dorothy Corona and Peggy Brewster.

Lauren Brewster and Marge Curran at Christmas Eve dinner n Oberammergau's Hotel Turmwirt.

Wayne H. Brewster

Berchtesgaden's Ramsau church.

Munich. View of the Oktoberfest park from our hotel window.

The Irascible Cherry Bomb

Schwangau church near Neuschwanstein castle.

2020

Patsy Cline

When you reach my age and can glimpse the Pearly Gates from where I'm standing, it forces you to look back and ponder life's blunders. The horrid realization struck me that my love life was one song short of a Patsy Cline playlist. I mean, I love Patsy Cline and all, but I didn't intend for my romantic life to end up as a country-western soap opera. Not that I ever meant it to be. It just happened. Maybe it all started because my Momma had the kitchen radio tuned to Phoenix's KOY every morning before I left for school. Len Ingelbrigtsen's morning show was her favorite, and he would spin those Patsy Cline songs, and they became ingrained in my brain. Let's review this trainwreck.

Typically, it all started as *Sweet Dreams* when *He Called Me Baby* but ended in *Your Cheatin' Heart*. Oh, I could name names, but I won't. Nor will I expose the tawdry sexual details as I don't want my readers to have the vapors. Let's state, I've walked

Photo from Encyclopedia Britannica

a long and winding romantic pathway, which always ended in *Heartaches*. A couple of times, I made the mistake of *Back in Baby's Arms*, but it turned out to be *Faded Love*. Time and time again, as new people entered my life, I would draw *Love Letters In The Sand*, thinking this time it was *True Love*. Then the arguments would start with them throwing *You Made Me Love You* in my face. After back and forth verbal accusations, I'd ask them, "Do you have *Leavin' On Your Mind?*"

Now don't start spouting your New Age poppycock; I've been through tons of therapy, Of course, I thought I was *Crazy*, but it turned out that I was fulfilling my need for codependent attachment. *Have You Ever Been Lonely?* Still, *I Fall To Pieces* thinking about those lost loves and wondering *Why He Can't Be You* in the persona of Mr. Right. Maybe Mr. Right doesn't exist, but I know I've had all the Mr. Wrongs that I can stand. I've had a lot of experience sending them all *Walkin' After Midnight*. Self-love is the safest love!

Patsy Cline, when we meet up in heaven, I'm fixin' to bitch slap you!

2020

Rice Krispies Treats are Life Sustaining

2020! *Anno horribilis.* This year, we're all struggling with life-threatening and vital issues: COVID-19, isolation, riots, equal rights with respect and dignity for all, overt racism, unemployment, economic survival, U.S. national elections, and the list goes on never-ending. It's been a trying and depressing year for most people. My problems pale in comparison to those listed above. However, I do have the Constitutional-given right to complain. And often do!

One ongoing issue has been a pain in my side since moving to Mexico eleven years ago. None of the supermarkets consistently stock the food items I want/need/desire/demand to maintain my privileged life. Let's review the list. Sigh.

There was an inconsistent availability problem with pumpkin puree that became a significant issue every fall, so when I stumbled across a can, I hoarded it until needed. As a result, I have dozens of large cans in my pantry that say best used by March 2018. Hmmm. I don't even know how to make a pumpkin pie, but I have the filling if I did.

The Irascible Cherry Bomb

Don't even get me started on non-existent Italian sausage. The last Italian sausage seen in Morelia was two years ago, and it's in my freezer, collecting a nasty case of freezer burn.

Now walk in my shoes and consider other beloved items next to impossible to find: fresh cranberries, red kidney beans, yellow wax beans, dried split peas, angel food cake mix, blood oranges, lemons, brown sugar, hazelnuts, molasses, and the list goes on and on—double sigh.

My family and friends have heard me bitch and moan about this subject for years. I've been so desperate for some of these items that I've smuggled them back in my suitcase from U.S. visits and paid outrageous extra baggage fees. When Mexican customs open my bags, it looks like I have toted an entire grocery store inside. Poor, pitiful, pathetic me!

The number one item that I always searched for and sniveled about was Rice Krispies cereal. I mean, how was I to exist in this foreign land without being able to make my Rice Krispies treats for special occasions? It is brutal, horrendous, sad, emotionally demoralizing, and any other drama queen term you can apply. I've stockpiled boxes of this cereal like they were gold. Finally, one store in town, Superama, brought some in for Christmas, and I bought four or five boxes, as I knew they would be gone and never seen again. So, much to my surprise this week, I discover that both Walmart and Mega have begun stocking this cereal. I almost had a heart attack in the cereal aisle! *"Clean up on aisle 12!"*

Now the other part of this equation, which is very problematic, concerns marshmallows. The packages here contain white vanilla-flavored marshmallows *with strawberry-flavored ones!* I have to buy multiple bags and separate the two kinds. I tell you, my life is a living hell.

My Mother's Rice Krispies recipe

1. Buy a box of Rice Krispies cereal.
2. Follow the recipe on the box.
3. Add shredded coconut and chopped pecans to the other ingredients.
4. Enjoy!

2018

Mother's Day Remembrances

Mother's Day. It is a day of holy obligation for most of us, but a holiday that generally doesn't lock into one's memory bank. I mean, they're sentimental, flower-festooned, Hallmark Card-designed celebrations, which don't evoke those crystal-clear moments you remember all your life. How can this holiday compete with the likes of Christmas and birthdays for emotional impact? There ain't no way, José! But within my lifetime, three Mother Days were exceptions.

I grew up in a small town, Glendale, Arizona. Back then, it was as Mayberry USA as they come. We had two weekly newspapers supported by a population base of 8,000 to 10,000 people. I imagine real news was hard to come by in our small town with the critical information reported through Phoenix's newspapers. After my mother died and while cleaning out her house, I discovered a chest of drawers crammed full of local news articles that featured our family and friends. Looking back now, she had faithfully collected these news stories for her four boys, and it was a cluttered snapshot of mid-century life in Glendale. There were snippets about family gatherings, birthday parties, visiting relatives, school achievements, scouting awards, sporting events, marriages, obituaries, church programs, on and on. I hate to admit it, but many of those clippings ended up in the trash. Although I am almost as much a sentimental pack rat as my mother, I did save more than a few of those news articles and have secretly stashed them in a closet at my son's house.

From that period, one relevant news story featured my sweet, red-haired grandmother, Daisy Brewster, as Glendale's Mother of the Year. I'm uncertain of the year as the date is missing from the clipping, but my best guess is 1955. I remember the extended family gathered at my Aunt Adelaide and Uncle Dale's home for a Sunday afternoon dinner to celebrate the occasion. It has stuck in my mind because it turned into a requisite photo opportunity, and the entire family gathered in the backyard and had multiple photos taken. Most of those photos exist in those hidden boxes in my son's closet but remain imprinted on my memory.

I believe it was the following year, my mother, Mae Brewster, was named Glendale's Mother of the Year. Why did our family have a monopoly on this honor? It beats me, but I do remember bits and pieces of this day very clearly. After church, the extended family gathered in our front yard to snap pictures in our Sunday best clothes. Corsages, more prominent the better, were evident and quite the norm for that time. The most memorable part of this day for me concerned the celebratory lunch. Thankfully, Dad didn't make my mother cook a meal at home, but he took the entire extended family out to lunch.

(Please note, my father wasn't cheap but tended to be very basic and frugal in his approach to life. This attitude meant that he didn't embrace eating out in restaurants. He always said, "Why spend money eating in restaurants

The Irascible Cherry Bomb

when you can be more comfortable eating at home?" Ugh. Even when we went on month-long vacations all over the United States, Dad found motels with kitchenettes so Mom could make breakfasts in the room. Some break for her! But, I digress).

The entire family walked two blocks from our house, crossing busy Grand Avenue and the railroad tracks, to La Perla Mexican Café. This iconic Glendale café existed then as a no-frills Mexican food provider and not a destination/celebratory restaurant. The punch line is that the La Perla-experience excited and impressed me. What can I say? I had a deprived childhood of low expectations.

The last memorable Mother's Day was in the early 1980s. My brother Ron devised a plan to celebrate this day at the Pinecone Inn in Prescott, Arizona, a drive less than two hours from our respective homes. Logistically, we drove two cars. My mother, Ron, and his wife Karla were in one that left from Glendale. My family and my mother-in-law Marge Curran motored from the East Valley to Prescott. We decided to take my mother-in-law's Oldsmobile, as it was more comfortable and safer than whatever car I owned at the time. Everything was fine until we started going up the little hill by New River. Her car started bucking, stalling, and finally quit right before the New River exit off I-17.

We waited for fifteen minutes, and it started. I drove to the only gas station in New River, and they couldn't help me, as there was no mechanic. We decided the wisest course of action was to head home. I called the Pinecone Inn from a payphone and left a message for my brother that we were having car trouble and would not make our reservation. We spent the entire afternoon nursing that car back to Tempe. It would start and then stall after a couple of miles. Repeat and then repeat. Frustrating for all of us as it was hot sitting and waiting for the car to start. And where did we finally celebrate Mother's Day? In a non-remarkable Mexican restaurant! I definitely did inherit some of my father's genes.

Retelling this tale of three Mother's Day celebrations concerning three remarkable women in my life—Daisy, Mae, and Marge—strengthens my love for them and their memory.

Grandma Daisy Brewster as Glendale's Mother of the Year, 1955.

The Irascible Cherry Bomb

*Mae Brewster on Mother's Day with other family members.
(Left to right: Elsie Smith, Mae, Adelaide Brewster, Daisy Brewster,
Margherite Brewster, Ida Brewster).*

Mae Brewster and Marge Curran.

2020

Skill Set

My friend Sid Foutz called me yesterday and, in a surprising testimonial to the COVID-19 quarantine and its subsequent effect on people, he proudly stated he had started baking. I dropped the phone!

You may say, "So what?" Everyone is baking these days as a sort of therapy for being in coronavirus prison. But when Sid tells you that he's in his kitchen and baking, then it must be the dawn of new world order. Let's delicately state that Sid's kitchen skills are a little underdeveloped. But, of course, I'm too kind. He readily admits he has a kitchen because it came with the house, which leads me to the actual story.

Years ago, during Phoenix's October Gay Rodeo, Sid threw a party that featured store-bought lasagna and salad. Okay, no shame in that. Three months later, he discovered a full cinder-block, coal-black lasagna in the oven when prepping for another party. I rest my case!

Hence my disbelief when he told me he was baking, which does require the use of the kitchen and specifically the oven. After

The Irascible Cherry Bomb

I recovered from the shock in our recent phone conversation, he told me he invented a bundt cake recipe, which he has perfected. "Really?" I said, not believing it for one second. "Yes," he stated, "You take a spice cake box mix and one small can of pumpkin puree, mix them together, add a few pecans, butterscotch chips, a little ground nutmeg, and bake it in a bundt cake pan." Now I've not tried this cake recipe, but he swears it's delicious. He did mention the word "dense" since he hasn't added eggs, oil, or water. It makes you wonder. I'm curious, does dense mean inedible?

If you want to try Sid's recipe, let your conscience be your guide as you've received my warning of Sid's "underdeveloped" kitchen skills.

2018

September in Mexico

September 15, 2011. Today is a historically significant day in Mexico. Two hundred-one years ago, Mexico declared independence from Spain, and the country celebrates this event with unabashed patriotic passion. Known as *Fiestas Patrias*, every building, car, and humble abode is adorned in the country's flag tri-colors—red, white, and green—giving this colorful country even more vibrancy. All of Mexico is in party mode. Every pueblo and city has a grand *fiesta* to celebrate this event culminating in *El Grito*, which was the call to fight oppressive Spain by Roman Catholic Father Miguel Hidalgo y Costilla in Dolores, Guanajuato.

Every September 15 at 11:30 p.m, the country's president steps out on the old Palacio Nacional balcony in Mexico City and repeats the exact words yelled two hundred years before. *¡Viva La Independencia Nacional! ¡Viva Mexico! ¡Viva Mexico! ¡Viva Mexico!* The crowd yells the same in a passionate patriotic response. Then the

The Irascible Cherry Bomb

president rings the bell calling the *paisanos* to action, as did Padre Hidalgo in the Revolution. It's an emotional experience for all Mexicans of every social level and origin. The next day, long parades feature all military branches, school bands, beautiful women in folk costumes, and handsome *charros* on horseback. During the two-day celebration, the vendors crowd the streets. They offer everything from shiny multi-hued balloons, colorful *Fiestas Patrias* memorabilia, tempting sweets of every variety, aromatic *tacos de carne asada*, and gigantic corn-on-the-cob smothered in mayonnaise, cheese, and dusted with *chile* powder. The aromas are intense and embracing, just like the mother country.

Additionally, the countryside has joined in this colorful fiesta. The abundant summer rains have transformed the dry and dusty landscape into a tapestry of every green hue known to man—olive, chartreuse, lime, Kelly, and evergreen. This earthly green draping is often parted by vibrant color, as if God had used a palette knife to smear vast swathes of deep pink, gold, orange, and lavender wildflowers. Steel-blue of agave fields and freshly plowed plots of ochre earth provide the occasional contrast. Dotting this landscape are giant prickly pear cactuses crowned with their ripe, ruby-red fruit. A cerulean sky frames this entire vista, often obscured by huge, humid clouds promising afternoon rains to tame the heat of the day. Ancient volcanoes rounded and smoothed by the passing time populate this *tierra*. But these ancient mountains add majesty to the land and remind us that it was not always a tranquil place. Each peak has a caldera that once spewed forth hot molten lava and deadly gases, but now, these soft mounds, clothed in low-lying clouds hiding the summits, only whisper mystery. Here and there, tiny pueblos are hugging the base of these hills. Each town has a church that stands high above the houses and businesses, their steeples reaching for the sky like arms outstretched in praise of God.

During September, the *milpas* are ready for harvesting the corn that is the staple of the Mexican diet for centuries. Where there is available land, the Mexicans have planted corn. Even within the city, vacant lots are mini-farms. But this is not unexpected, as Mexico is a land of contrasts. Mexico is both ancient and modern. She continues to live with one foot firmly planted in the 21st century and the other foot in time past. Some farmers still bring their harvests to market on the back of *burros*, as they have done for centuries. These tiny animals trudge down the urban streets with heavy burdens while the Mercedes Benzes and BMWs swerve to pass safely. You learn to accept this diversity as it's part of the DNA of Mexico.

Life moves slower here, and with it, change. And in many ways, it offers a better quality of life than our larger neighbor to the north. Only God knows what is in store for Mexico during the next one hundred years of independence. I pray it brings peace, prosperity, and political stability to this beautiful country. *¡Viva Mexico! ¡Viva Septiembre!*

2020

A Bridge Too Far

Bridge. A once-popular card game that evolved from whist in the nineteenth century. One that I like to call masochistic archaic torture. Some delusional people still enjoy playing the game, live and in person, and I was one of those individuals until recently.

Here's the problem with this game. There are too many rules and bidding conventions, and some players take it way too seriously.

I took up the game in the 1970s. You know what I mean, a few drinks, friends, food, conversation, and then play a few hands of cards. My approach to the game became bedded in that concept. Bridge equaled fun times with friends.

After a thirty-year hiatus, some well-meaning ex-pats *desperate* for a fourth player invited me to join in weekly bridge afternoons. The group included an Oxford-educated genius who played the game at a master level. Can I spell i-n-t-i-m-i-d-a-t-e-d? The gods fated disaster and humiliation.

The Irascible Cherry Bomb

Initially, Mr. Oxford and the other two people forgave my ineptness, but as we continued to play, their expectations of me rose. I do admit that I tried to remember all the conventions. For example, if your partner opens bidding with two clubs, it means that they have twenty plus points, which is half the points possible. It would be best if you used the correct Bridge-speak to let your partner know what's in your hand. You better not screw it up or daggers suddenly get thrown your way.

I never mastered this requisite language and had to dodge a lot of daggers. Of course, it would be much easier stating in English what exists in your hand, but this is called "table talk" and is strictly verboten! So I occasionally went with my gut in my attempt to play the game.

My creative responses didn't sit well with my fellow players. How can I politely describe their reactions? Let's say the daggers turned into machetes to detach my head from my body permanently.

Then there were those fellow players who loved "critiquing" my play. One of them used a calm, diplomatic approach, while another amped up their rock-concert-voice for the hard of hearing. This Person's shrieking voice reverberated off the walls, vibrating my body, and dislodging my dentures, that is, if I wore dentures.

I was on the receiving end of This way-too-competitive Person's teaching more than I care to remember. I mean, at the end of the day, it's only a game. It all became more stressful than fun, so I quit. I hung up my hat. Adios. Adieu. Auf Wiedersehen.

I'm not the only one. The game is in a steady decline without attracting new players. "Hey, Millenials, would you like to learn to play bridge?" Uh, no! It doesn't take a genius to figure out that this game will pass into history, much like buggy whips and corsets.

My guilty pleasure is still playing bridge online but without the threat of decapitation!

2017

Cold Soup

It's summertime! We're all looking for relief from the heat and searching out refreshing recipes to enhance our dining repertoire. Salads are ordinary, but cold soup is extraordinary. One classic soup conjures up elegance and sophistication, but it's a blend of humble peasant ingredients. Vichyssoise is cold potato and leek soup. But done well, it's sublime.

Much debate concerns the exact origin of this soup as being of French or American heritage, but, according to my research, it seems to be from both countries. As the story goes, Chef Louis Diat worked in New York City's Ritz Carlton Hotel in 1917 and tried to come up with a cold soup to serve his guests. His thoughts went back to his youth in France, where his mother would make him a stew of potatoes and leeks. But he and his brother would always add cold milk to the hot soup, as they loved it in this form. Therefore, he set about creating a version of his childhood soup that would be cold. *Voilà!* He invented Vichyssoise, named for Vichy's French town, which was close to his childhood home.

Now when I think of Vichyssoise, I think of my first Thanksgiving as a married man. Peggy and I lived in San Francisco in an elegant old high-rise building on Russian Hill. We were very young and very naïve but were feeling quite sophisticated residing in San Francisco in such a beautiful neighborhood. Our first significant holiday separated from family, we were determined to celebrate it in style and panache beyond our means and definitely beyond our culinary skills. Peg's mother graciously sent Peg's sister, Edie, for a visit so we wouldn't feel so lonely. We devised an elegant menu that began with Vichyssoise and progressed to roasted duck. Well, since neither of us knew anything about cooking, it turned into a meal from hell. Poor Edie hated everything and would only eat the Jell-O lime salad that had turned out well. Despite this culinary train wreck, I still love Vichyssoise but haven't eaten duck since.

Here is a recipe that I've made many times to rave reviews. You may serve it hot or cold. My sincere wish is that your results are much more memorable and pleasing than ours were that first Thanksgiving.

Potato and Leek Soup
(Recipe courtesy of Emeril Lagasse)

1 large or 2 small leeks

2 bay leaves

20 black peppercorns

4 sprigs of fresh thyme

2 tablespoons butter

2 strips bacon, chopped

½ cup dry white wine

5 cups chicken stock

The Irascible Cherry Bomb

1 pound of russet potatoes peeled and diced
1 ½ teaspoon salt
¾ teaspoon white pepper
½ to ¾ cup whole cream
Finely chopped thyme for garnish

Make a bouquet garni of two leek leaves, bay leaves, peppercorn, and thyme in a cheesecloth bag. Set aside. Trim the leek(s) to just the white and light green portions. Cut in half and wash thoroughly to remove any dirt within them. Slice thinly crosswise and set aside.

In a large soup pot over medium heat, melt the butter and add the bacon. Cook for 5 to 6 minutes, occasionally stirring until the bacon is very soft and has rendered most of its fat. Add the chopped leeks and cook until wilted, about five minutes. Add the wine and bring to a boil. Add the reserved bouquet garni, chicken stock, potatoes, salt, and white pepper. Bring to another boil. Reduce the heat to a simmer and cook for 30 minutes or until the potatoes fall apart and the soup is very flavorful.

Remove the bouquet garni and process using a stick blender, or working in batches, puree the soup in a food processor or blender. Stir in the cream and adjust the seasonings. You can rewarm it gently or serve it immediately. Or, if serving it cold, refrigerate until ready to plate. Sprinkle the chopped thyme over the soup before serving.

September 7, 2007

Dawn of a New Day

It was early morning, and the rising sun was clear and bright. Its rays were casting golden hues on steel-gray clouds creating a majestic primordial scene. Puddles—left by the night's thunderstorm—were scattered about the tarmac and reflected this natural beauty. While looking out the large plate-glass windows in front of my departure gate at Phoenix Sky Harbor International Airport, I reflected on my impending journey. My U.S. Airways' flight destination was Guadalajara, Mexico. How could I've realized that this dawning of a new day would be life-changing?

I was departing Phoenix for a well-earned vacation and was visiting parts of Mexico unknown to me. An adventure. Yes, I hoped this trip would involve some exciting experiences, but I was also looking at my retirement locations. Although, many years in the future, I hoped to one day retire to Mexico and open a small retail store.

Predictably, the previous night's monsoon storm had been brief but fierce, with the usual combination of lightning, wind, and rain. There's nothing like an Arizona summer monsoon for natural drama. The only damage done was that it knocked out the power in my neighborhood, which meant no air conditioning the whole night. (To Phoenicians, air conditioning is one of life's essentials, akin to food, water, and Bermuda shorts. Whenever this happens, you suddenly realize that your whole life revolves around electricity—phone, lights, television, microwave oven—and most importantly, home climate control. During these electrical blackouts, all you can do is open all the windows and pray that you can create a cross-breeze.) As the hours passed, the hot, sticky natural air did nothing to aid my night-before-trip anxiety and sleep.

This situation reminded me of stories that my father told me regarding his life in early 20th century Phoenix. It was customary for everybody to have sleeping porches as part of their homes during this pioneer-period in the desert. They dampened sheets to help them sleep through the hot summer nights. These stories gave me a renewed appreciation of their pioneer perseverance and how far removed I am from my family's Arizona roots. This morning, I was excited about my adventure but felt the undercurrent of grogginess and uncertainty. Thankfully, the recently purchased Starbucks' *grande*, shade-grown coffee-of-the-day helped diminish my sleep deprivation and awakened my inherited pioneer spirit to the task of exploring new territories.

As I watched this dramatic scene unfold outside the terminal, it triggered my mind to consider the worldly symbolism of dark and light. Impetuously, I thought, would my first solo vacation turn into scrapbook-perfect golden memories or dark, nightmarish experiences? I quickly brushed aside those childish thoughts. For decades, I traveled alone on countless business trips, but

I never ventured on vacation without the company of a close friend, life partner, or family member. How could I possibly have anticipated what awaited me traveling alone for ten days in a foreign country?

I speculated that solo travel is very different for a sixty-year-old man than for a twenty-something backpacker. My hard-earned years have taught me to be a little more cautious and appreciative of a bit more luxury. I've traded in those youth-hostel years for something more akin to three or four-star luxury hotel years.

With retirement looming in the future, I wanted to see if there were locations in Mexico where I could live comfortably and start a new life. For months I studied guide books, magazine articles, online blogs, and maps to plan this trip. Through my years of involvement with Mexican friends and boyfriends, they consistently mentioned Michoacán as the most beautiful state. They called it the Soul of Mexico. This poetic reference intrigued me. Therefore, I planned to spend most of my time in Morelia, the capital city, and the nearby Magic Pueblo[1] of Pátzcuaro. For added interest, I included a side trip to Valle de Bravo, another Magic Pueblo, in the state of Mexico.

Onboard, I found my assigned window seat 2A. I loved to view the passing scenery below and tried to imagine what it looked like

---

1. Magic Pueblos of Mexico. Developed by the Secretary of Mexican Tourism in 2001, this program designates town that possess historical, architectural or cultural significance. Each town receives federal funds to improve infrastructure, repairs and publicity. Now there are some 40 towns with this special designation scattered across the entire Republic. The program has been successful with increased tourism and economic development for most participants.

The Irascible Cherry Bomb

at ground level. On the short three-hour flight, I watched as the various climate zones passed below. They changed from the arid Sonoran desert to the rugged, mystical, and immense canyons in Chihuahua and Durango. Sinaloa's verdant, fertile farmlands shifted to Nayarit's subtropical, densely forested hills and finally to Jalisco's temperate highlands.

On approach, we circled north of Guadalajara, and I was surprised to see multiple large waterfalls cascading into a deep canyon. Was this a national park or simply rain runoff dumping into the ravine? The urban sprawl was shrouded in smog and made me think of Los Angeles before emission controls. As we landed, the most startling fact became evident, the size of the airport. The terminal looked more appropriate for Bozeman, Montana, rather than the second-largest city in Mexico. This impression was the first of many discoveries of Mexico compared with its larger neighbor to the north. Our plane parked on the tarmac, unable to secure a gate. We deplaned and boarded a bus for the short trip to the terminal.

I quickly passed through passport control, then waited for my luggage to be delivered. Another lasting impression happened during this time. At the baggage claim, strangers approached me and engaged me in conversation. This engagement wasn't a scam but Mexican friendliness. (If this happened in the United States, we'd feel that the person was trying to invade our privacy, but Mexicans feel no hesitation in commencing a friendly and curious conversation. Many times the questions are too personal, and you do twitch and squirm before answering.) These fellow travelers appeared sincerely interested in why I was visiting their country and where I was going.

Finally, the luggage arrived on the conveyor belt, and there was a mad scramble by everyone to grab their bags and make their way towards the Customs agents. I saw my bag and hauled it off the conveyor. I approached the unruly crowd as each individual seemed intent on trying to be first through Customs. I stood back in amazement and laughed. I've experienced this previously during visits to Spain, Portugal, and Italy. Call it a cultural difference, northern European-based cultures stand patiently in line waiting their turn, but Latin cultures tend to push and shove their way forward. I shouldn't generalize, but this crowd was an unorganized, soccer-skirmish-fashioned pack that spoke very loudly to their travel companions while jockeying for position.

Spanish had suddenly replaced English in my existence. I silently kicked myself for taking German and Latin in high school. My street-learned Spanish was only going to take me so far on this trip. Getting the rental car was developing into a confusing experience as I had only the slightest understanding of the contract terms I signed. The insurance cost two times more than the car rental, but I'd have been responsible for every single peso of replacement value without the insurance. I love taking risks, but going without insurance would have been terminally stupid.

"Is there a map available of Guadalajara?" I asked the rental agent. "No," he responded. "Could you please give me directions to the toll road that goes to Morelia?" "Of course!"

Now I listened to his instructions in Spanish and felt a little bit out of my element. I wasn't jet-lagged, but it seemed more like complete language immersion without a life preserver. I listened and asked a few more questions. Okay. After a positive affirmation of "I can do this," I hopped into my Nissan Tsuru with a manual transmission, then jerked and shuddered my way out of the parking lot. All the while, I thought of John Candy's car in the movie *Uncle Buck*. All I lacked was the backfiring belch of smoke.

After negotiating a roundabout while dodging *kamikaze*-driven buses and taxis, I finally headed in the right direction. I immediately took the first exit pointing the way to Lake Chapala and Morelia. Of course, this was the wrong exit and the free road to Morelia. A slow and panicky realization hit that it would take almost eight hours to drive to Morelia if I stayed on this road.

Naturally, I stopped numerous times and, in my halting Spanish, asked for directions to the toll highway. The elusive answers varied with each stop and did nothing to solve my problem. My frustration was mounting, and the hundreds of *topes*, ubiquitous Mexican speedbumps, on this two-lane road only added to my angst.

In the town of Ocotlán, I received some good news. A kind lady told me to find a particular street and continue north until I found the highway. I would find an entrance there. I let out an audible sigh of relief and thanked her for her help. Okay, I located what I thought was the street, and I continued north out of Ocotlán. Hurrah. I spied the toll road ahead. Suddenly, I passed over it without seeing any entrances. I stopped and carefully turned around on this narrow road without any shoulders. Now I drove slowly over the toll road looking for any sign of an entrance. On both sides of the road were *milpas*, cornfields. Wait, what was that? I spied a primitive dirt road on the side of one of the fields, and it appeared to go to the shoulder of the expressway. I decided to take it as it was my only option. It was rough, and in my little car, I felt every rock and pothole in this pathway as I bumped along. Within a few seconds and in a dust cloud, I found myself leaving the highly illegal access road and safely entered the toll road. I didn't care if I had just broken my first Mexican law. The relief I felt was akin to being released from prison for my crime of being a stupid Gringo.

The remaining trip through the countryside was pleasant enough, although a bit disappointing. It was predominantly agricultural without any picture postcard scenic vistas. I saw fields of blue-green agave that would eventually become tequila or mezcal, enough cornfields to make you think you were in Iowa, and giant prickly pear cactus that are an iconic symbol of this country. For me, the most intriguing factors in the landscape were the dry stone walls surrounding the fields. I thought of all the back-breaking labor exerted to clear those fields and stack the stones. But I had hoped to see some charming, picturesque villages. And where were the sombrero-bedecked men riding tiny burros, and *Lupita* in her embroidered peasant blouse--lowered seductively over one shoulder while drawing water from a well? Isn't this our visual image of Mexico? We trapped those images in our heads for the generation of Americans who grew up watching Zorro and The Cisco Kid on television. I expected to find the legendary country of haciendas, fiestas, and Pedro tilling the fields with his oxen. But the world changed, and along with it, Mexico. Mercedes and BMWs zooming past me are the new reality on this contemporary *Camino Real*.

As I got closer to my goal of Morelia, the landscape became greener, with profuse wildflowers on each side of the road. Additionally, the flat agricultural landscape transformed into multiple volcanic-shaped mountains, and I drove in a late afternoon rain shower. As I came over a hill, I spotted a large body of water. I was surprised and confused since my guidebooks made no mention of this vast lake. Later, I found out it was Lake Cuitzeo. I was amazed by the size and beauty of this lake nestled at the base of tall hills. There were numerous small and non-descript villages dotting the shoreline. I saw fishermen out on the lake in flat-bottomed launches or *pangas*. There were hundreds of white ibis wading in the shallow lake or flying to fresh fishing or nesting sites.

Finally, I came upon the exit for Morelia. This *salida* was quite a few miles north of the city proper and took twenty minutes before I entered Morelia. I had reservations at a modest motel, Villa del Sol, for the first night. I accurately thought it would be easier to find the motel on the highway versus trying to find a hotel in the inner city. I pulled into the parking lot. I felt rather smug, having accomplished the navigation to Morelia despite the trip's first half debacles.

Once I checked into my room, I opened the windows to let in the fresh evening air. I laid down on the bed and reflected on what a delight this was after last night's sticky, hot Phoenix air. My lungs took in a deep breath, and I exhaled with a sigh of pure contentment. But shortly, I noticed swarms of mosquitoes had entered the room. So much for my period of tranquility! I jumped up and closed the windows. It might have been nice if the motel owners had thought enough of their clients to put screens over the windows. The rainy season in Morelia birthed a bounty of blood-sucking insects, and they all found their way into my room. This predicament was my penance for rejoicing in the cool weather. I leaped around my room, batting away at these pests with my Fodor Mexico guidebook as my weapon of choice. Finally, satisfied with the carnage, I decided it was time for some dinner. After a quick and non-memorable meal at the hotel's restaurant, I took a nap in preparation for enjoying Morelia's nightlife.

Around 9 pm, I got up, showered, and changed into some fresh clothes for my evening out. I got a taxi and asked the driver to take me to a club called *Con La Rojas*. As we made our way to Morelia's center, I was stunned by the city's architecture and beauty. The buildings constructed from pink cantera stone are in colonial baroque style, which made me believe I was in Spain or Italy. My head spun in every direction, trying to take in as much as possible. The city glowed from all the flood-lit historic buildings with narrow, cobblestoned streets lighted by sizeable wrought-iron lanterns. The scene was so charming and magical that I felt I had made the right decision to visit here.

The taxi turned onto *Calle Aldama*, a side street of buildings hugging narrow sidewalks. Stopping, the cab driver indicated the entrance and address of my destination. The nightclub's doorway was nondescript with no prominent signage or marquee. It appeared more like a residential entrance than one for a popular disco. I paid the cover fee and walked the short hallway towards the interior. Once into the main area, I was stunned by the tasteful décor and transformation from a former colonial residence into a 21st-century nightclub. What was once the interior courtyard had become the dance floor with the usual high-tech lighting and sound systems suspended overhead. Off the dance floor were various rooms that now housed the bar and seating areas. These individual rooms featured oversized Spanish Colonial style

The Irascible Cherry Bomb

decor of tables, altars, religious art, lighted candles, and assorted accessories. Pin dot halogens subtly lighted the *objets d'art*. I was immediately impressed by the originality and tasteful presentation. I was guided to a table in a small room with an opening facing the dance floor. On the wall to my left, a large oil painting of Our Lady of Lourdes watched over the festivities, and I thought perhaps she would perform a miracle for me tonight.

The waiter who showed me to the table requested my drink order. Of course, he was young and handsome. After requesting a beer, I asked, "What's your name?" He responded, Ivan. But what impressed me as the night wore on was his attentiveness to his customers and his warm personality. Without being too pushy or over the top, he was sincerely devoted and quick to produce another drink or bowl of snacks. He kept bringing me a shot glass full of a liquid. I tasted it thinking it might be a form of *pulque* or some other exotic liquor, but couldn't identify it. After drinking three beers, I finally asked him what the liquid was. He responded, *"Jugo de limón."* Pure lime juice! Another embarrassing Gringo lesson learned! I consciously acknowledged that Ivan had made the night an incredible pleasure. He was the first person I met in Morelia, and he made a positive and lasting impression. I hoped that his tips from other guests were commensurate with his level of professional service.

The clientele at *Rojas* was a mixed diversity of young gays, lesbians, and straights. Although it was labeled a gay club, it attracted a group of people who loved energizing music and a comfortable, safe atmosphere. The evening's entertainment started with a couple of drag numbers. Naturally, I assumed it was a local drag queen performing, but some other customers quickly informed me that the performer was the owner and a *Mrs.* Opps! What's the adage about assumptions? *Ass-u-me.* The D.J. volumed-up the incredible sound system, and the floor became a frantic mass of erratic movement. I sat and watched these youthful and lithe participants feeling every year of my age. They were all energetic and seemingly happy. Somehow I missed this youthful "club" stage of life. I married young and was never a bar-scene type of person. But in the last ten years or so, I've experienced this lost part of my life, just a little later than most.

After many hours of mind-numbing techno beat and too many *Dos XX Lagers*, I decided to call it a night. I said my goodbyes to Ivan and placed a generous tip in his hand. Making my way around the crowded dance floor, I approached the entrance/exit. I saw the owner seated on an oversized throne-like chair surrounded by lighted candelabras. Queen was the first word that came to mind, so I bowed and thanked her for a lovely evening in her club. A bizarre ending to a very long and memorable day.

As I drifted off to sleep, I remembered thinking of how life-altering this first day had been. Morelia had instantly captivated me with her beautiful architecture, European-ambiance, and friendly people. Had I discovered my perfect place to retire? Perhaps.

2020
Epilogue

My life finally led me to live in Morelia, beginning in June 2009 or almost two-years after my first visit. Two more subsequent visits during that space of two years made me decide that Morelia was my ideal retirement place. Unwillingly, the Great Recession forced me to move up my timetable for retirement from U.S.

business. I must state that I've never regretted the move. Morelia continues to enchant me with her glorious weather, historical surroundings, incredible diverse countryside, and varied cultural activities.

I look back at my naiveté during that first day and feel somewhat embarrassed. I've traveled extensively through North America, South Pacific, and Europe during my lifetime, so I'm not a neophyte to new experiences. One of the joys of discovering new places is the newness and differences in cultures. Now I'm a blasé ex-patriot who takes many of these differences as my norm.

My first overseas travels were to the south Pacific, which led me to believe I would like to live in Australia. That didn't happen, but marriage, family, and work did. But there was always that dream tucked away. Then life allowed me the pleasure of knowing many Mexicans within Phoenix and their home country. Little by little, my brain formed the idea that Mexico would be a great place to live. Unfortunately, most U.S. citizens lack an accurate understanding of Mexico and life here, and I was no exception. We tend to think of poverty, cartels, deserts, and beaches as signifying all that is Mexico. How unfortunate that most of us miss an enlightened view of what is current-day Mexico. It is modern and yet retains one foot firmly planted in its historical past. Morelia, founded in 1541, existed long before any European culture on U.S. soil.

In retrospect, living in the Soul of Mexico is a dream come true. The experience has enriched my soul and expanded my perspective. Morelia was my destiny!

2016

The Saga of the Blue Kitty

Once upon a time, in a land far, far away, there lived an older man who dreamed of a blue kitty. The blue kitty was a classy Persian breed with puffy powder-blue fur and the faintest of smiles on its face.

Upon awakening, the older man realized that the cat's powder blue fur doesn't exist in nature but only in his dream. This dream puzzled the older man for several reasons. First, because he never remembered his dreams in his youth, and now, with old age, he recalls them all too clearly. Secondly, the dream's subject matter was unusual because the older man is highly allergic to kitties and can't bear to be near them. Finally, it seemed strange to the older man that he would be dreaming about a blue kitty. What did it all mean? He set off to find an answer to this strange vision.

First, he contacted his sage former wife. "Former wife, what do you think my dream about a blue kitty meant?" he asked. The former wife replied, "It means you're turning heterosexual!" The older man carefully examined that response and thought, perhaps, former wife was not all that wise. Then he researched this question in the Dream Bible. Sure enough, there was an entry on blue cats. It said that a dream about a blue kitty is a positive illusion or delusion. "That's a possibility," he said to himself, since he often lived in a state of delusion. Reading further, it stated that "people who believe in past lives or the supernatural quite frequently dream of blue cats." "Hmmm," declared the older man. "That is thought-provoking." So, he began discussing this with his closest friends in the far, far away land, and they all thought it was interesting, too.

Weeks passed, and the older man often thought of that dream and the blue kitty. Then, during a journey to the Magic Pueblo of Pátzcuaro with one of his dear friends, Susan Tucceri, an unusual event occurred. She purchased a gift and gave it to the older man. It was a sugar figure of a blue kitty to be used as a part of the Day of the Dead celebration. Eureka! At that moment, it all came together for the older man, and he knew that the blue kitty represented his longing for his family and friends that have departed this mortal life. Or so he hoped.

Time passed while the older man labored intensely on a second novel centered on the real and fictional life of his cousin, Keith Van Zante. As the story evolved, Keith became a CIA spy masquerading as Aart van Krusen, a Dutch diplomat, working in the West German Dutch embassy. The older man learned that CIA spies were assigned letter codes to designate their location through extensive research. For Aart, his code letters would be BL = The Netherlands and CA = West Germany. Shocked, the older man wondered if this was a coincidence or fate. It seemed apparent that his cousin's code name would be the Blue Cat.

About the same time, and in a related twist on this theme, the older man and his formerly sage ex-wife stumbled upon a Prescott, Arizona bistro, *El Gato Azul*. (Spanish for The Blue Cat and the couple were pleasantly surprised how good the food was.) It was becoming evident that the sun and stars had aligned to reveal the true nature of the older man's dream. It was beyond coincidence and now seemed like destiny.

The dream was guiding the older man on a path of discovery and enlightenment. The moral of the story is: Dream big. It could change your life for the better.

Maybe blue Persian cats do exist!

December 1989

The Spicery Christmas Eve

Christmas Eve, a perfect night to express affection for our family, to forgive those who failed you, and to forget past mistakes. –Unknown

Christmas Eve 1989, I'll never forget it. I've long ago forgiven my brother over the thirty-one-year-old incident. May he rest in peace, my brother Ron was long on great ideas but short on execution. Bless his heart! He possessed many excellent characteristics of passionate public service, humor, a positive outlook, and family love. Unfortunately, he didn't think through objectively, plan accordingly, or anticipate the difficulty in achieving his goals. When he would involve me in his "Lucy" cornball schemes, I became "Ethel" with pie smeared all over my face!

In 1989, Martha Campbell bought our parent's Glendale, Arizona home and was in the process of turning it into The Spicery restaurant. Ron got the bright idea that the extended Brewster family should have one last glorious Christmas Eve in the house, and I should be the one to facilitate it. Brilliant! Nostalgic! Disastrous!

On December 23rd, my former wife Peggy and I met Ron and his wife Karla to decorate the old house for Christmas Eve. The place was a train wreck! It was an active construction zone.

There was no electricity. There was no heat. There was no hot water. Sawdust and plaster powder, an inch deep, covered everything! There was hardly any furniture. And there was no kitchen for me to use in preparing an elaborate dinner for thirty people. Oh, my dear Christmas Carol nightmare! How were we going to change this "Bah-humbug" situation into a joyful venue for a party? Ron failed to see any problem with this! I wanted to shoot him if I'd owned a gun. And if only wounded, Peggy would have finished the job for me. We were both so disgusted with him!

We immediately started an intensive cleaning that took hours to complete, as filth covered each piece of furniture, the curtains, the floors, every window, nook, and cranny. We dusted, scrubbed, and polished. We set up borrowed chairs, tables with tablecloths, and enough plates and drinkware to serve everyone. Decorating was the next business order, and Peggy and I had this covered. Ron's one responsibility was to provide us with a beautiful Christmas tree that would be the focal point of the night. Of course, he had found the world's ugliest Christmas tree. It made the Charlie Brown Christmas tree look full and lush. I was furious! I gave him money and told him not to come back until he found a six-foot Noble fir tree that matched my expectations. I then butchered the ugly tree for greenery and placed it strategically around the rooms. Solved that problem! We filled the living room and dining room with countless candles for light and warmth. After working all day, the final product looked festive and pretty. Thank god, Peg and I owned and brought extensive party supplies, tableware, and decorations to make this event possible.

The cherry on top of my Christmas sundae was the issue with no kitchen and no electricity. How the hell was I supposed

The Irascible Cherry Bomb

to serve and feed all these people an elaborate gourmet dinner? Ron's answer—run the world's longest extension cord from our Aunt Adelaide's house across the block, through a former bedroom's window, and heat everything in a low-wattage microwave. Holy Master Chef! I precooked everything in my home and then transported it twenty-six miles from Mesa to Glendale, where I reheated every element in a tiny microwave. It was a slow, frustrating, and laborious process to get food on the table that frayed my holiday nerves beyond my usual Tiny Tim cheerful limit. Scrooge had it easy compared to my Spicery Christmas Eve experience.

According to some attendees' recent comments, it was a glorious last Christmas in our parents' home. Go figure! It's one holiday that I'll never forget!

2019

Erin Go Bragh

Ahh, the luck of the Irish!
I've just returned from a short trip to the United States. As is my custom, I purchased a ton of various items, which are difficult or impossible to locate in my country of residence, Mexico. (You might be inclined to mock me for my wacky ways, but believe me, my family did a thorough job of that before my departure.) Here is an abbreviated list of said items: taper candles in seasonal colorations, a perfect artificial floral bouquet for the guest bathroom, delicious Godiva chocolate instant puddings, new fat man clothing, luxurious bath towels, themed party supplies, Blu-ray DVD player, critically needed decorative pillows, and well, you get the picture. Perceived essentials for my exiled life.

I crammed all these treasurers into two suitcases the size of steamer trunks and two carry-on bags. I can hardly afford the extra baggage fees, let alone manage to maneuver all the cumbersome luggage through the terminals. However, my greatest challenge is clearing Mexican customs. (This has been a lifetime

The Irascible Cherry Bomb

fear ever since my first trip to Europe. I got caught smuggling into the US an 18 karat gold Italian bracelet for my then-wife Peggy.) Fortunately, on previous occasions returning to Mexico, I pressed the customs button and received a green light to proceed without inspection. This time I wasn't so fortunate. I pushed that little button, and I received the dreaded red light! My heart jumped up into my throat, and my stomach revolted in sympathy. Then began the task of manhandling these unwieldy coffin-like bags onto a waist-high stainless-steel table for an agent to inspect. I grunted, and I heaved, and maybe even farted a bit, while the agent stood by watching this scene unfold. Now I'm sweating and looking guilty of every imaginable crime while doing this. The unsmiling agent unzipped the first bag and lifted the flap. What greeted her was a giant, green-metallic, tinsel shamrock. Her eyes bugged out in surprise. I imagined she was expecting high-end electronics, but instead, a good ol' Irish shamrock smacked her in the face. I casually said, "I bet you don't see one of those every day!" She laughed and said, No!" This surprise broke the ice, and the inspection ended.

Thanks to the luck of the Irish, I wasn't imprisoned or fined for abusing the importation limit. God bless the Irish!

2010

A Travel Story: Four Young Men and One Senior Citizen

The true story of a weekend adventure in Zihuatanejo

Author's Note: In 2009, I moved to Morelia, Michoacan, Mexico, to begin a new life as a retail shop owner. My only friend when I arrived was another gay man who owned another retail shop. We became best friends, and Eduardo introduced me to other gay men within the community. I felt compelled to impart a tiny bit of backstory to this misadventure.

I asked myself, *"What was I thinking?"* Of course, this was after the fact, and after I have once again experienced a memorable life lesson. This hindsight provided me with crystal-clear vision even without the aid of my progressive trifocals. Why would a 62-year-old man accept an invitation to accompany four young gay men in the prime of their lives to a weekend at the beach?

It started with a phone call from my friend, Eduardo (37 years old), asking if I wanted to go to Ixtapa/Zihuatanejo with him and his boyfriend, Pablo (23 years old). "Sure," I said without the slightest hesitation, as I was ready to do anything to break my dreary routine of work, home, and sitting alone on the weekends. They were my best friends in Morelia, so there was no concern

The Irascible Cherry Bomb

about traveling with them. As I was making the reservations for a hotel, Eduardo called and informed me that another friend, Ronaldo (33 years old), wanted to come with us and bring his off-again, on-again boyfriend, José (24 years old). "Well...okay," I replied meekly. I did have some doubts at this point, but as I said, I was *desperate* to do anything to get out of the house, even if it meant sharing a room with two people that I didn't know well. Once I make up my mind, I generally plunge in with both feet. No backing out!

The trip to Zihuatanejo from Morelia was beautiful and took about four hours. We passed through four climate zones and ended up in a tropical paradise with lush foliage and exotic, colorful flowers everywhere. It reminded me of Hawaii but with a Mexican flair. Nothing unusual had happened so far. We checked into the hotel and went to our rooms to change clothes, with our mutual goal of getting to the beach and having a celebratory piña colada. In preparing for the beach, I bathed in my usual SPF 64 sunscreen and put on my beach garments that could have existed in a 1920s Miss America beauty pageant but were useful in hiding my sagging body parts.

On the other hand, my roommates changed into their beach attire. Speedos! OMG! I thought only Olympic swimmers, Acapulco cliff divers, and Greek Gods wore those, but somehow Speedos had become the Official Gay Young Man's Beach Attire. I don't know how I missed that memo from the LGBTQ (the ultimate ruling body of our community), but I did. Naturally, with their entire bodies exposed, I got a close look at their skin. Damn! It was too perfect! Taunt and olive and *not a blemish anywhere!*

On the other hand, my skin had enough defects to resemble the moon's surface, and we won't even mention the incredible creping effect taking place on my legs and arms. This situation undermined my already low self-esteem! (Admittedly, I have lived in denial for the last few years. Every day I'm surprised to see in the mirror that I'm wearing the mask of an older adult. Inside I am still a contemporary of these young men, but outside I look like I am ready for a Fright Night party.)

Well, I decided, if I had come this far, paid for the hotel room, and bathed in sunscreen, I might as well get over my insecurity and shuffle out to the beach. Of course, I was the first in our little group to arrive because they were still gathered in front of the mirrors adjusting their "property," mousse-ing their hair into perfection, and selecting the right masculine accessories to accompany their beach attire. I chose a front-row palapa on the beach and aggressively waved to the waiter for service. I needed a piña colada, and I needed it now! Alcohol was the answer to boost my confidence level. Finally, the others arrived along with my drink—there we were: four bronze hunks and one lumpy bag of white flour reclining in chaises on the beach! I'm sure many people saw our group and said to themselves, "What the heck are those handsome young men doing with that old geezer?"

After my numerous creative denials for not entering the water with my travel companions (that would have meant exposing my skin to them), Eduardo decided that we needed to take a launch across the bay to Playa Las Gatas to have dinner. Only then did I learn how we had to get to the boat situated about 50 yards offshore. (*Hello!* Here was another life lesson!) We had to get aboard

The Irascible Cherry Bomb

one of those horrible yellow rubber banana boats that you see everywhere on the beach. (I'm sure you know the ones that I mean? Those horrendously uncomfortable floating devices that they drag behind a speeding boat, and they slap the waves like a hand on a desk while the people hang on for dear life. You can hear the women, children, and presumably, gay men screaming in sheer terror across the entire bay!) Well, I had no option but to climb on this awkward vessel to get out to the anchored boat. Getting on one of these rubber rafts is an easy task when you are young and supple, but when you are over sixty, it requires a lot of *chutzpah* and a lot of helping hands pushing and shoving you into place. Not very impressive if you are trying to convince the others in your party that you are "young at heart!" The only positive thing about this experience is that we didn't capsize either time in the loading and unloading process. Ultimately, we did have a nice dinner on the beach, but then the terror began again. We had to return to our hotel in the same manner as we arrived. My friends were heaving and ho-ing like they were pulling a whale carcass into the boat. How humiliating!

After surviving this life-threatening experience once again, we arrived back at our hotel, where Eduardo announced that we needed to get cleaned up to go out to the disco. Since I was the chauffeur, there was no way I could have given them some lame excuse like," My shrimp tacos are starting a party in my stomach" or "I have to do my weekly manicure tonight." Instead, I nodded my head and smiled, despite my inner-soul preferring my cozy bed to what awaited us at the disco. Thankfully, I had packed my hottest club outfit for this occasion: a youthful long-sleeved shirt, relaxed jeans with the right amount of distressing, and some stylish black loafers! I took a quick shower and got dressed, and I was feeling pretty good about myself. I'd lost twenty-five pounds over the last few months and could almost detect a waistline again. Of course, that was until I saw the club attire of my travel companions. They were wearing cool t-shirts that fit their tight little bodies like second skins. Of course, no fat is allowed on a gay man's body. At this point, I hated them all and planned how I could kill them and dispose of their cute bodies. But being a good sport, I held my head up and sucked in my stomach (as much as I could) and walked out with them, secretly hoping we won't be able to find a gay bar in Zihua.

Being neophytes to Zihua's gay scene, we had to ask twelve different strangers on the street before finding out any information on these bars' exact location. The *"party"* street runs behind the Pollo Feliz (Happy Chicken) fast-food outlet. (Somehow, that seemed very appropriate.) Unfortunately, the only two gay bars in existence sat on the same block as the type of bars you hear about in Tijuana, Nogales, or Juarez. Just walking by them and looking at the patrons made me believe that those people would never make the sexiest men (or women) alive lists. The bar we finally entered, Club Maribel (the best gay club in town) as the other "club" was closed for the night. Thankfully, there was no cover charge as I would have felt violated if there had been! You had to climb *dark* concrete stairs to the second-floor club. These stairs were so steep and narrow; they were almost like a ladder. Of course, there were no handrails or security strips on the stairs as this is Mexico, and human safety is of little concern here. My companions scampered up them like they were giving out prizes for arriving safely. I was groping my way up a-step-at-a-time and

The Irascible Cherry Bomb

holding on to the wall in false security, thinking it was a semi-stabilizing force. One wrong move and I would have been a crumpled heap of old skin and bones at the bottom. Luckily, I made it up without incident. Then I had the opportunity to look around at the ambiance and "décor." The only unifying theme going on in this club was butt-ugly highlighted with black lights. Zihuatanejo is known for heat and humidity, and before smartphones and TripAdvisor, we only discovered after the fact that Club Maribel had no airconditioning. Well, imagine how pleasant the climate was inside this closed bar. But the best part of the decor was the furniture. The owner had a great idea on how to save space and get more people into the bar. He decided *children's furniture* was the logical solution. Here we sat on chairs that even my grandson would have found too small. Can you imagine grown people drinking and smoking while sitting around small "activity tables with matching chairs?" It was like a scene from a Woody Allen movie or maybe even an Edvard Munch painting. I felt like the "Silent Scream-er" sitting there, hoping the night would end soon. If it had been my decision, I would have left after the first warmish beer and after watching an obese cowboy with a giant beer-belly trying to dance with his *two* lesbian girlfriends. But no! My friends insisted on staying until after the first drag show at one a.m. Luckily, we left after the last fat drag queen did her three-song homage to Rocío Durcal (Spanish singer/actress and Diva). On the way out, one of my friends asked what time they closed. The waiter answered, "Seven in the morning." How could anyone sit in those horrible chairs all night? Maybe there was a second shift of patrons, drunker and uglier. I shuttered even to imagine that scene.

So the next time Eduardo asks me to go along for a weekend outing, I will be asking a lot of questions. Unless I am still *desperate* for entertainment, I will utter the same unthinking and naïve, "okay!" Damn the consequences!

The cast of characters.

2015

On the ocassion of Valentine's Day

Is it just me, or have you noticed that after you take down all the Christmas decorations that our environments look dull, void of color and, might I even say, depressing? Well, it's my humble opinion that Valentine's Day solely exists to prevent us from becoming overly depressed and consequently committing mass suicide. Think about it. All those shiny sensuous red hearts, fragrant vibrant roses, and massive doses of tryptophan-filled chocolate are just what any naturopathic psychologist would prescribe!

Not everyone over-decorates for the holidays like yours-truly, but after that final garland comes down, I stand there frozen in the cold, barren wasteland that my home has become. No more twinkling lights or glittering icicles hanging on the railing and no more retro bubble-lights gently effervescing on the Christmas tree. Hence, a few days later, I am frantically looking for my red honeycombed-foldout hearts and strands of heart-shaped lights, like the strung-out holiday junkie that I am. I can't rest until I have redecorated for the special day of love and friendship. Finally, with splashes of color here and there, I'm at peace.

My first real recollection of this holiday happened when I was in grade school, probably Miss Logan's first-grade class. I remember the homework assignment to create a decorated "mailbox" to receive Valentine's cards from my classmates. Additionally, Miss Logan requested us to buy those tiny individual cards for each of my classmates. (You all remember the type with the cutesy sayings, like *"rose are red, violets are blue, and I can't live a day without you!" Talk about early co-dependency messages; no wonder I can't have a healthy relationship.*) I'm sure my mother helped me with the mailbox project, and the end-result reflected our lack of refinement and creativity. It was an old shoebox that we covered in red construction or crepe paper on which I glued miscellaneous symbols representing the holiday, with the glue-stain-marks adding certain panache. I carefully selected cards that I thought "proper" for each classmate, with my favorite chums receiving the cutest. When the actual day arrived, I carefully carried my homemade mailbox to school and eagerly anticipated it filled with delightful cards. Other details have long ago escaped me, but I know I was thrilled to be participating in the act of giving and receiving these simple symbols of friendship.

After I was married, I learned how important this day was to my new wife, Peggy, and my in-laws. They celebrated it al-

The Irascible Cherry Bomb

most like a second Christmas. My mother-in-law, Marge, was a notorious "holiday-aholic" and shopaholic. Every holiday was a reason for a special celebration. For February 14th, she made sure each family member received numerous Valentine-themed gifts that she had carefully selected and beautifully wrapped. She would also create a special dinner menu to make the day extra important. But her desserts were always *le pièce de résistance*: heart-shaped red velvet cakes artfully decorated with icing flowers and flourishes; mini cream puffs (*profiteroles*) drizzled with bittersweet chocolate; or giant chocolate-covered strawberries. I sure miss Ol' Marge! Over the years, the celebration moved to our house, and we had to perform at the same or higher standards set by my mother-in-law. So my holiday over-indulgence comes from a long history of family association. It is a learned behavior.

The custom of sending mushy messages to our "chosen" one dates back to the Middle Ages. Naturally, the English couldn't be so bold as to come right out and state their feelings, so they developed elaborate cards to express their most passionate thoughts. In the United States, Ester A. Howard, of Worchester, MA, created the first commercial Valentine's cards around 1840. She received her first Valentine's card from England and decided to start hand-making these cards from real lace, ribbons, and brightly colored pictures called "scrap." Therefore, the USPS has Miss Howland to thank for the almost one billion Valentine's cards sent each year.

After seeing the stationery industry's success, some other sectors got the bright idea to participate in this cash cow. Now the candy, floral, and jewelry industries are enjoying their second Christmas, and our guilt is forcing us to join in this sentimental commercialism, subconsciously knowing it is good for the economy. To not participate would be downright un-American and un-romantic. Wait a minute, since 70% of all US cut flowers come from Colombia. Maybe it is un-Colombian! And then I thought of Godiva and Lindt chocolates, but they come from Belgium and Switzerland. And diamonds come from Africa. I guess if we didn't participate in this Valentine's Day frenzy, it would un-Worldly!

After all the hype, the best gift of all is the true sentiment of love and friendship. So this year, I send each of you sincere wishes for a day filled with love, life, and laughter.

Happy Valentine's Day!

2012

A State of Mine

K ansas.
 I hear the word Kansas, and instantly my heart warms. It might not hold the same panache as New York or California, but this heartland state possesses true grit, American values, and vibrant history. This state of mine grabbed my soul and won't let go.

I bet some visual images of Kansas come to mind. Perhaps, the Great Plains, those endless flat prairies that extend uninterrupted to far-off horizons, pop in your brain. Sometimes, I see the winter wind blowing so stiff and unyielding that I imagine Kansas snowdrifts ending up in Missouri. Or how about sprawling wheat fields rippling in a warm summer breeze? Then, movies and television have done a mighty job of portraying Kansas. I can't forget Nellie Forbush's song from the musical *South Pacific*, with the memorable lyric of "corny as Kansas in August." *Gunsmoke* brought frontier Dodge City, Marshall Matt Dillon, and Miss Kitty to life through many successful television years. Nor can we forget the influence of *The Wizard of Oz*, Dorothy, and Auntie Em played against a black and white Kansas backdrop in that colorful iconic movie.

We must scratch below the stereotypical surface to find depth and character. Beyond corn and plains, Kansas contains significant industry, vibrant culture, fabulous universities, lively cities, and a good old-fashioned dose of Americana. Noteworthy citizens proudly called Kansas home: Amelia Earhart, Hattie McDaniel, Milton S. Eisenhower, and John Cameron Swayze, to name a few. More importantly for me, my parents set forth into life from humble Kansas beginnings. Their strong roots bound them and our family to this land called Kansas.

Both of my parents[1] were born into farming families that resided near Thayer and Earlton's small towns. Through different life paths, they both ended up in Arizona, where they met, married, and produced a family of four boys[2]. As in many historical migrations, once one family member moved west, other family members followed. After WWII, we were a family firmly divided into Arizona and Kansas contingents. Every summer of my youth, we would make a pilgrimage to visit those Kansas relatives. It was a journey home for my parents—full of eagerness and excitement—to reconnect with family. Like the debris scattered by a tornado, southeastern Kansas held our remaining relatives. They lived in towns with strange-sounding names—Chanute, Parsons, Wichita, Thayer, and Neodesha—but when I hear these words,

The Irascible Cherry Bomb

they bring forth a feeling of well-being and recognition. Those town names also trigger recollections that helped to define me.

We would stay in our families' homes during these visits, which presented some unusual challenges for me. Several of our relatives still lived on farms and carried on a lifestyle that was utterly foreign to this city boy. At Uncle Ralph and Aunt Alma Robertson's farm, I remember having to help collect eggs and being extremely frightened of the nesting hens trying to peck me. Aunt Alma would try to calm my fears and show me how to reach under the hens to extract their eggs, but I never did master this chore because I felt guilty stealing those hens' eggs. Likewise, Uncle Ralph tried in vain to teach me how to milk a cow. I must admit the memory of drinking that unpasteurized milk still activates my gag mechanism. But there were fun times as well. On many occasions, my young cousins came to visit their Grandma and Grandpa Robertson. We explored the barn during their visits, jumped into the hayloft, and swung on a rope hanging from the rafters. A broad creek bordered the farm, where we pestered snapping turtles with sticks.

Aunt Alma & Uncle Ralph Robertson with Ron & Wayne.

My Grandmother, Daisy Belle Brewster, was a Smith before she married Archie Brewster. Her siblings consisted of two brothers and one sister divided equally between the Kansas and Arizona divisions. Daisy and Archie moved to Arizona in 1912. In quick succession, her brother, Ed, moved to Glendale and had an adjoining farm. Uncle Will remained in place, along with the remaining sister, Rena.

Uncle Will Smith's farm sat just down the road from Uncle Ralph and Aunt Alma's. It was an essential visit for both my mother and father, and it requires an explanation. Uncle Will, Daisy's brother, was my father's uncle. Uncle Will[3] lost his young wife, Catherine[4], to influenza leaving behind a son, Neal, and two daughters, Thelma and Wilma, to raise. My mother, recently divorced[5] and in need of work, took on the job as Uncle Will's housekeeper. She worked there for approximately ten years but ultimately decided she needed a change. Daisy came to visit her brother one year—probably around 1930—and persuaded my mother to go to Arizona and work for her. My mother leaped at this chance, and in due course, she met my father, and they fell in love. This double connection between my mother and father with Uncle Will Smith demanded that we spent several days visiting his farm.

In 1933, tragedy struck this family again. Uncle Will's eldest daughter, Thelma, was the teacher at Brewster schoolhouse. She was driving home one afternoon and perhaps had her mind on a box supper to take place that evening. Thelma had to cross a raised train track alongside the main highway to reach their family farm, and we can only speculate why she didn't heed the approaching train. The local authorities called her father, and he helped pull his daughter's body out of the wreck. Meanwhile, Wilma was attending the state teacher's college at Emporia, and her father called her home. Wilma stepped in and taught her sister's students at Brewster School for the rest of the term.

The Irascible Cherry Bomb

Wilma remained on the farm with her husband, Forrest "Smiles" Chickadonz, and their two girls, Nadine and Modine. The extraordinary circumstances that brought my mother and Wilma together formed a special bond between them. Of course, through marriage, they were now cousins. Only now do I realize what a special relationship they had. Visiting their farm created some unforgettable memories for my siblings and me. I loved riding their big red horse named Ginger, while my older brothers enjoyed fishing in the farm's stocked pond. The most frightening memory of these visits happened when a massive, snorting bull chased me as I walked along the pasture's fence.

During our 1950s and early 60s visits, I encountered a primitive, rural lifestyle, including crank telephones, hand-pumping water from cisterns, chamber pots, and outhouses. Everyone had extensive gardens, which meant fresh vegetables and fruit during the summer months with lots of canning to preserve the bounty. The amount of constant and exhausting work to maintain a successful farm remains daunting for me. Naturally, many other relatives left farming and moved into town to engage in more lucrative and less labor-intensive occupations.

Aunt Rena (Smith) Powell held my most beloved Kansas relative status, and I wasn't the only one who thought so. She garnered affection from everyone that knew her. In retrospect, her life was both ordinary and extraordinary.

Rena lived alone in a comfortable little bungalow with a full front porch in the town of Neodesha. During the 1950s, this town thrived as a picturesque mid-American town with a busy commercial Main Street and quiet tree-lined residential neighborhoods. On our annual visits, the excitement built as Dad drove down Main Street and then turned left, heading south for a few blocks on Aunt Rena's street. Our car's wheels turning over the town's brick-paved streets created a cadence that I can still hear. In my mind, it sounded like a horde of hornets buzzing their angry protest at our interference. Once we arrived, all of us leaped out of the car, and there would be Aunt Rena standing at her front door with her sweet smile and open arms welcoming us.

Aunt Rena's house graced an ample corner lot at South 3rd and Mill Streets, across from the town's hospital and near a bluff overlooking the Fall River. Two large oak trees dominated the front yard and shaded the west side of the house. She maintained a vegetable and flower garden in the rear yard that produced corn, zucchini, tomatoes, lovely peonies, gladiolas, and zinnias[6]. At the tail end of the plot stood an arched wooden trellis covered with a rambling red rose that always seemed to be in bloom. Adding an architectural element to the back yard was a multi-level wren house painted white with red trim.

Country Hospital across from Aunt Rena's house.

The house's most essential and distinctive feature was the gabled front porch with its twin wooden porch swings[7] facing each other. After dinner, we would retire to those swings to escape

The Irascible Cherry Bomb

the hot interior and try to catch a cooling breeze. Conversation, while we slowly rocked, became a natural activity during those peaceful moments.

I remember seeing fireflies for the first time. Growing up in the Arizona desert, I'd never seen or heard of these insects and had to ask my parents what they were. Those fascinating flying creatures would twinkle and flitter across the darkness. My brother, Ron, and I experienced the youthful summer tradition of chasing the fireflies and catching them in glass Mason jars.

Aunt Rena maintained the inside of her house sparkling clean and comfortably furnished. The interior's fresh yet full fragrance has haunted my memory over the years, a unique combination of oak, lavender, and fir. One impressive feature in her living room caught my youthful attention; the very first RCA color television I'd ever seen. It seemed like a miracle to watch those early programs in color during our visits.

Aunt Rena possessed a charismatic personality that stood out in sharp contrast to her sister's, my grandmother. Daisy tended to be reserved, serene, and quiet. Aunt Rena spoke more and acted in a manner, which I would call spunky. She showed interest in all aspects of life and enjoyed interacting with everyone. Her petite stature enhanced her impeccable yet conservative clothes. She never left her house without gloves and a hat. I can still see her pulling on her gloves and adjusting each finger's fit with the other hand.

When she walked, she would take more significant steps than her small frame would naturally allow, which gave her a striding-like appearance. Her movements were quick yet lady-like. Then abruptly, she would stop, turn, and place her right hand on her hip to discuss a particular point of conversation. Sometimes she would punctuate her dialogue with the free left hand, pointing towards the person she was speaking to and cocking her head to one side while waiting for a response. Reddish-brown hair adorned her head, which, through the years, turned more white. She tried to control her hair's wiry structure via a tight bun and numerous bobby pins, but somehow, her hair would escape and create a loose halo around her face.

Aunt Rena with Fred Rollin on their front porch.

Aunt Rena's joyful nature masked a tragic family life. She married Fred Powell, and they had a son, Fred Rollin. Aunt Rena brought her mother, my Great Grandmother Anna Smith, to live with them. Fred, Fred Rollin, and Anna all died within three years and left her alone for twenty-eight years.

Uncle Fred Powell died in 1942 from a heart attack. He remains a mystery to me since no one living can provide any insight into his personality. An old family archive photo showed Fred as a rotund man standing in front of his house wearing a heavy wool suit, vest, and a felt fedora hat. Generally, people remembered that he loved to smoke cigars and play poker. For years, he held the job of Neodesha postmaster. Aunt Rena always swore that the cigars killed him, but at this point, only God and Uncle Fred know the cause.

Fred Rollin joined the Army during World War II while a student at the University of Kansas. He became part of the 191st Tank Battalion as a Second Lieutenant. This battalion saw massive action against the enemy in North Africa, Italy, France, and Germany. They suffered more losses of tanks and men than any other corps in any war or operational theater ever in the annals of our history. Unfortunately, Fred Rollin gave the ultimate sacrifice of defending his country, killed in action on October 26, 1944[8], in France. His body rests in The Epinal American Cemetery, Epinal, France. With these three[9] losses in such quick succession—mother, husband, and son—Aunt Rena must have been emotionally devastated. Perhaps her strong faith, friends, or family support brought her through those dark days. Somehow she survived this trauma and moved forward with grace, strength, and humility. She never played the victim or seemed sad to those of us that knew her best. She didn't seem to dwell on the past but appeared confident and in control of her life.

My father adored Aunt Rena. One summer, he begged her to accompany our family on a road trip to the East Coast—including stops in Boston, New York, and Washington D.C—and we made a pilgrimage to the national park at Valley Forge, Pennsylvania. Within this park stands the beautiful, Gothic-styled Washington Memorial Chapel with its Patriots Tower. Covered within the tower's interior surfaces are many small brass plaques commemorating U.S. soldiers fallen in the line of duty. Our primary reason for our Valley Forge visit, Aunt Rena desired to locate Fred Rollin's name memorial, which she had commissioned for inclusion in this monument. Once she found the plaque, I can still visualize her and how emotional she became, weeping openly. Only now can I understand her pain, grief, and sense of loss regarding Fred Rollin's death, which surfaced during this visit.

Frisco train station, Neodesha, Kansas.

During the war, Aunt Rena and a few other women in Neodesha started a City Canteen to provide food, magazines, and entertainment to soldiers passing through town on the Frisco Railroad[10]. These patriotic women convinced the stationmaster to give them part of the luggage room for this purpose. They also successfully rallied the town's merchants in helping them get provisions for the soldiers. In all, some 200,000 soldiers were entertained by this little canteen during the war years, which is an impressive number for little Neodesha, Kansas.

Somehow Aunt Rena and Grandma Brewster shared the same tastes when it came to breakfast. As a child, I had enough natural curiosity to ask them what they were eating and drinking, since it was nothing I had ever seen. Whether at home or on the road, their standard breakfast was a cup of Postum™ and several slices of Sahara Desert-dry Melba toast. Postum™ no longer exists as a supermarket brand because I assume their customers all died off, and the younger generation discovered the world of great-tasting coffee and tea. This coffee-alternative beverage, made from wheat and molasses, wasn't a flavor marriage made in heaven. There is a reason Starbucks exists on every corner instead of Postum™ cafes!

Right after Christmas, Aunt Rena would climb on a train and headed west to visit her Arizona family. Her arrival began a several-month stay in relatively warm Arizona during the bitterest months of a Kansas winter. During these months, countless family gatherings happened within relatives' homes. More significant in my memory were the Sunday desert picnics that my Dad planned. These were large family affairs involving every relative living within the greater Phoenix area and featured potluck platters of food, real campfire-brewed coffee, pleasant conversation, and long walks through the desert.

I remember most clearly one picnic that took place on New Year's Day in 1958. It was significant for numerous reasons. It was the only time my father selected a spot overlooking the Verde River, which is now a planned community named Rio Verde. Secondly, my two brothers, Leonard and Rex, brought their fiances, Janie Miller and Arlyn Moores, to the picnic, and this meant a new beginning and change of dynamics within our family. Aunt Rena attended, so she must have left Neodesha directly after Christmas to be with us that day. That day's group photograph still hangs proudly in my house and represents a time of hope, new adventures, and togetherness for our family.

Kansas held a diminished interest for most of my teen and adult years. After I entered high school, the annual Kansas summer trips ended for my parents and me. Our Kansas relatives began passing away in rapid succession. Others moved to other parts of the country for jobs or maybe just for a new life. But year-by-year, there were fewer and fewer reasons for my parents to return every summer.

Aunt Rena struggled with some health issues through the mid to late 1960s. Finally, she was no longer able to care adequately for her house or herself. She entered a nursing facility that had just been constructed directly across the street from her home. Ironically, she spent her last days of life gazing towards her now-vacant house. She passed away on March 6, 1970, at the age of 88.

My mother made a solo trip to her funeral as my father had just passed away the previous October. Other relatives and friends from all over the U.S. packed Neodesha First Methodist Church for the service to mourn the passing of this great lady. She never achieved fame or fortune or a footnote into history. But she created something even greater during her life. Her legacy speaks of the boundless love, admiration, and joy she gave and received from everyone that knew her. How can we measure the effect that her life had on us? We can only speak from the heart that her presence made us feel extraordinarily special and loved.

So when I hear the words, Kansas, Neodesha, Aunt Rena, I am transported back in time to days, people, and places that mattered. Kansas remains an essential state of mine.

The Irascible Cherry Bomb

Aunt Rena in her garden with the rose arbor.

Aunt Rena in the desert during an Arizona visit.

Desert picnic with Aunt Rena (1950).

WAYNE H. BREWSTER

Another desert picnic: Rex Brewster, Mae Brewster, Leonard Brewster, Aunt Rena Powell, Ron Brewster, Aunt Alma Robertson, Lyle Robertson, Howard Norland, Ruth Robertson Norland, Ralph Robertson, Grandma Daisy Brewster, Uncle Will Smith, and Margherite Brewster.

New Year's Day 1958: Rex Brewster, Frieda Moores, Arlyn Moores Brewster, Janie Miller Brewster, Aunt Rena Powell, Leonard Brewster, Grandma Daisy Brewster, Margherite Brewster, Adelaide Brewster, Ron Brewster, Dale Brewster, Ida Brewster, Uncle Loren Kinne, Harold Brewster. Missing from the photo were Mae Brewster (taking the picture), Truman Brewster and Wayne Brewster.

The Irascible Cherry Bomb

January 1st gathering at Grandma Brewster's house: Mae Brewster, Adelaide Brewster, Uncle Ed Smith, Leonard Brewster with Sassy, Aunt Rena Powell, Rex Brewster, Grandma Daisy Brewster, Ronald Brewster, Dale Brewster holding Truman Brewster, Uncle Will Smith, and Elsie Smith.

Modine Chickadonz, Wayne Brewster, Nadine Chickadonz, and Ginger.

WAYNE H. BREWSTER

NOTES

1. Harold Lyman Brewster was born December 3, 1899, in Thayer, and Elsie Mae Leonard was born June 11, 1899, in Earlton. They were married September 3, 1932, in Glendale, AZ.
2. Leonard Lyman, b. July 24, 1934; Rex Eldon, b. December 1, 1935; Ronald Gary, b. August 14, 1940; Wayne Harold, b. April 5, 1947.
3. Will Smith was born 1873 and married Catherine Robertson. They had three children: Neal (b. 1899), Thelma (b. 1910), and Wilma (b. 1912).
4. Catherine was a Robertson and was an aunt to our Uncle Ralph Robertson. So the Smith, Robertson, and Brewster families are all connected via marriages.
5. Mae Leonard (our mother) married Otis Carnahan on June 3, 1918, before the Justice of the Peace in Erie, Kansas. Mom didn't stay in this marriage very long and the divorce was final in October or November 1919. I, nor my brothers, ever learned Mom's reasons for leaving him. Otis died within a year of the divorce being final. It remains a mystery and sad chapter in Mom's life.
6. Aunt Rena had a neighbor, Mrs. Thurber, who would help her with the garden. She lived across the alley directly north of Aunt Rena's house. I remember her as being very friendly but not very attractive due to some uncontrolled facial hair.
7. When Aunt Rena passed away, Ron indicated that he would like to have one of those porch swings. So one was shipped to his home in Arizona, and he proudly displayed it on his porch. After several decades, Arizona's dry weather destroyed the wood to the point of non-repair and it literally fell apart. Now the porch swing lives on in memory, but he cherished that swing for almost three decades.

8. He received the Purple Heart posthumously. Jean-Marie Siret of Frémifontaine, France, and a member of the association "la mémoire de Frémifontaine" took on the honorable task of maintaining Fred Rollin's grave and the site of the battle. He erected a plaque in memory of Fred Rollin and Pvt. Agapito Barraza (of New Mexico) that was also killed in the tank. I had found Jean-Marie's website several years ago and had sent a message, which he answered allowing me more knowledge and insight regarding Fred Rollin's death.
9. Rena's mother, my Great Grandmother Anna Smith passed away in 1941.
10. St. Louis and San Francisco Railroad served the middle US from Louisiana to Missouri and never got farther west than Texas. It ceased to exist in 1980 when it became a part of the Santa Fe, Atchison and Topeka Railroad.

Author's Acknowledgements

"Life imitates art far more than art imitates life." — Oscar Wilde.

Certain personal life events became stories for this book. So in my case, art imitated life more than the reverse. I've strived to make all the stories entertaining via humor, irreverence, or nostalgia. I hope my efforts engage you.

I wish to publicly thank those that have helped me with this current journey.

- Peggy Brewster, my former wife, connected me with this book's editor. Peggy also served as my go-to sounding board regarding the various subject matter and a host of questions in general. She has good-naturedly allowed her name to surface in many stories contained in this book.
- Mike Schermerhorn mentored me, corrected me, and encouraged me throughout the editing process. Profound gratitude and thanks for his professional guidance.
- Óscar Uriel Villalón Jacuinde designed an intriguing cover for the book. I have worked professionally with this creative designer for over a decade and am always thrilled with his work.

- León Felipe Herrera once again has produced the digital and print manuscript page layout for this book. He is a technical genius and continues to amaze me with his talent and knowledge.
- Mary Newell Bass—my long-term friend and former colleague—thank you for your consistent and emphatic pushing for me to publish these stories. You are the reason this book exists.
- Thanks to all who appear featured in this book. You were the spark to set off the creative process and have enriched my life with your friendships.

Table of Contents

The Irascible Cherry Bomb	1
Books, Food, and Sex: Escapes from Reality!	4
Car Issues	9
Cartalk	14
Weather or Not	19
A Meaningful Historical Date	23
Watch out for falling cows!	28
Christmas Musings	30
Want List	37
Clueless!	39
Dining Out - Deprivation and Recovery	42
Tik Tok or Not	53
Rethorical Questions	60
Day of the Dead	63
Household Tips and Other Tips	70
Dreaming of Paradise	72
Labels Suck!	85
March in Morelia	88
Places of Plenitude	90
Horsefeathers!	

Feast Day of Guadalupe	**100**
Latkes	**104**
European Christmas Vacation	**107**
Patsy Cline	**120**
Rice Krispies Treats are Life Sustaining	**122**
Mother's Day Remembrances	**125**
Skill Set	**130**
September in Mexico	**132**
A Bridge Too Far	**136**
Cold Soup	**139**
Dawn of a New Day	**142**
The Saga of the Blue Kitty	**154**
The Spicery Christmas Eve	**157**
Erin Go Bragh	**160**
A Travel Story: Four Young Men and One Senior Citizen	**162**
On the ocassion of Valentine's Day	**169**
A State of Mine	**173**

Author's Acknowledgements

Made in the USA
Coppell, TX
14 September 2021